The accidental Instructional Designer

Cammy Bean

ASTD Press is an internationally renowned source of insightful and practical information on workplace learning, training, and professional development.

ASTD Press
1640 King Street Box 1443
Alexandria, VA 22313-1443 USA
Ordering information: Books published by ASTD Press can be purchased by visiting ASTD's website at store.astd.org or by calling 800.628.2783 or 703.683.8100.

Library of Congress Control Number: 2014934634
ISBN-10: 1-56286-914-0
ISBN-13: 978-1-56286-914-4
e-ISBN: 978-1-60728-407-9

ASTD Press Editorial Staff:
Director: Glenn Saltzman
Manager, ASTD Press: Ashley McDonald
Community of Practice Manager, Learning Technologies: Justin Brusino
Associate Editor: Melissa Jones
Editorial Assistant: Ashley Slade
Text and Cover Design: Lon Levy

Printed by Versa Press, Inc., East Peoria, IL, www.versapress.com

Contents

Acknowledgments

While it's true that I have dreamed of writing a book since I was little, it's another thing to find that I have actually just written one. And it's certainly not a journey that I took alone, so I do need to take a moment now to thank the Academy. . . .

First and foremost, I would not be here without the mentoring, encouragement, and support I've received from my team at Kineo, where I have worked as the VP of learning design since 2009. Steve Rayson took that first chance on me, and there's been no turning back. Stephen Walsh sets the tone for everything I write. Steve Lowenthal pushes me to be better, always—even when I don't want to. Mark Harrison provided firsthand mentorship and inspiration.

Many of the ideas and content in this book are drawn from the Kineo website, where we've posted more than eight years' worth of insights on effective learning design. So much of what I share here comes from conversations I've had, or thoughts and ideas first put forth by those I've mentioned and other members of the Kineo design team including Matt Fox, Paul Welch, Catherine Jones, and Kirstie Greany. I'm just giving voice here to their brilliance, so they should be getting all the credit.

To my Kineo U.S. team, you collectively help me put these ideas into action every day and make them all better in the execution. Seriously, guys. You complete me.

To the many clients I have had the privilege to work with over the years—thank you for the opportunities, the challenges, and the collaboration. We are better together.

Ellen Wagner, a mentor and friend, listened to what I had to say, encouraged me to share, and gave me confidence that I had something worthwhile to contribute. Along with Jane Bozarth, Jeannette Campos, Janet Clarey, Koreen Olbrish Pagano, and Trina Rimmer—you women are the wind beneath my e-learning wings.

When I was too scared to let anyone read early drafts, Meghan Young persistently offered and let me know I was on the right track. Thank you!

So many of you good e-learning people have pushed me along in this journey through blog posts, books, tweets, presentations, articles, or late night conversations, and for that I thank you: Michael Allen, Julie Dirksen, Karl Kapp, Judy Katz, Tom Kuhlmann, Connie Malamed, Cathy Moore, Clive Shepherd, Aaron Silvers, Kevin Thorn, Reuben Tozman, Will Thalheimer, and Clark Quinn. You inspire me.

When Bill Brandon at the eLearning Guild published my first article, "The Accidental Instructional Designer," in *Learning Solutions Magazine*, I was thrilled, to say the least. Over the years, I have had the good fortune to speak at numerous eLearning Guild conferences, testing my ideas and hearing the stories of my peers. Thank you David Holcomb and Heidi Fisk for continuing to have faith in me.

ASTD, I am grateful for the opportunities you have given me to speak at conferences, help with conference planning, and for publishing my work. Justin Brusino, thanks for believing in me and getting this book off the ground. Melissa Jones, you dotted my "I"s and crossed my "T"s and helped make this book better than what it was.

To Susan Keyes Morrison, my mom, friend, and role model, you always make me feel like I'm more. Thank you.

The biggest thanks of all go to my family—Jon, our three kids, and our three pet ducks (who joined our family quite intentionally last summer). You managed to survive a couple seasons of me working late nights at the kitchen table on this book. For that—and everything else—I love you.

Cammy Bean
February 2014

introduction

Once Upon a Time

In this chapter . . .

- How did I go from a little girl signing in the shower to a grown-up woman working as an instructional designer of technology-based learning solutions?

- Do other people have similar stories?

- Is your story all that different?

A Walking Accident

I am a walking accident. Generally a happy one, but an accident nonetheless.

Most of my life feels like an accident—a series of unexpected events that have led to this particular moment in time. I look around and say, "How did I get here surrounded by these people, living in this state, in this house? How did I end up doing what I am doing?" This is not at all what I imagined. Or is it?

When I was a kid, I had visions of fame as a singer (while singing loudly in the shower, I hoped that our neighbor, who I imagined was a record label producer, could hear me).

I aspired to be a writer. In 1979, my sixth grade teacher Mrs. Shimamoto asked the class to write our personal predictions for the year 2000 (and, wow, was that a long way away). In my short story, I painted a picture of my future self as a work-from-home author with two children. They would eat a lot of Cheerios and I would write novels and magazine articles. Turns out this picture isn't all that far off, although it took me a few extra years to get here, there's an extra kid, and I have yet to write that novel. But I AM writing a book!

At some point, I also began to picture myself as a teacher. After majoring in English at college, I applied to get a master's in education, but that was something I never got around to after discovering the joys of a regular paycheck.

But by no means did I ever imagine that one day I would be an instructional designer of self-paced, online e-learning programs. Never. This was a complete accident.

Of course, in 1979 I don't think anyone had even said the words "e-learning" out loud yet—at least not in my presence. And I had certainly never heard the words "instructional design." It wasn't until 1996, when I got a fancy business card that said "Junior Instructional Designer," that I even knew such a thing existed. And even then it seemed sort of made up to me.

My Path to Instructional Design

So, how did I get here? I graduated from college in the middle of a recession, with a degree in English and German studies. I moved to Boston with friends to do the young-adult, livin' in the big city thing. I looked for work. I temped and taught swimming. I had idealistic notions of making the world a better place. Eventually, I landed a job at a company that helped employees of corporate America balance their work and family lives through referrals to child care and elder care services. I worked behind the scenes, running reports and helping employees figure out more efficient ways of working.

We did everything by paper in those days but the computer had definitely arrived. We started designing a new call center computer application for the company. I translated user requirements to the IT department. We designed screens and workflows. We decided what buttons should be called and did paper prototypes. Then, because I knew the system, I trained all the call center agents and counselors how to use it. I was good at it. I led classroom training sessions, updated workbooks, and wrote newsletters and tip sheets.

Eventually I started looking for a new job. Through a friend of a friend, I found out about an emerging multimedia production company that created CD-ROM training programs to teach people how to use software and other work-related skills. I would write scripts and produce video and, wow, it sounded glamorous. Thus, in 1996 I found myself with the fancy job title, "Junior Instructional Designer," and voilà, an instructional designer was born!

So, that's how it happened. And, most likely, it's not that different from your own tale of accident and intrigue; that day you woke up to find yourself responsible for designing instruction. My guess is that you didn't dream of this career when you were in sixth grade either. Am I wrong?

What I Did

There I was in this glamorous multimedia world—writing scripts and learning about learning objectives. We mostly created software training, following a pretty simple model: instruct, demo, practice, assess. A talking head video on the left side of the screen acted as the host, explaining basic concepts as text bullets appeared on the screen. That was really advanced back then, mind you. This was followed by a narrated animated software demonstration, a try-it-yourself exercise with guided instructions and feedback, and finally a test where you had to do it all by yourself.

This was in the days before e-learning authoring tools and standardized templates. Every screen was hand coded and an hour of computer-based training (or CBT as we called it) ran for $40,000 as a standard pricing structure.

At the time, I developed a somewhat vague notion that people went to school to learn about educational technology and we even had a couple of people in the company who had master's degrees in it. Fancy. But for the most part, we were just a bunch of smart people trying to do what seemed like cutting-edge stuff and make a living at the same time.

I worked there for about five years before the company evaporated in the dot-com burst in the early 2000s. I wandered off to massage therapy school and took anatomy classes and learned about the psoas muscle and how to give a really excellent therapeutic massage. I even ended up teaching massage for a few years (talk about hands-on training). All the while, I stayed connected to the learning technology business through freelance projects. It was a pretty cool life—I felt like I had figured out this magical balance between my more intellectual business side and my inner-healer. Then I started having kids and the reality of supporting a family hit home. I went back to full-time work and found a job as a senior instructional designer at a small e-learning company.

It was kind of a watershed moment, really. At that point I realized that, in all likelihood, instructional design might be my professional focus for the rest of my life. I could sit back and just do my job or I could make a commitment to do it with great intention and great passion. I chose the path of intention and it has made all the difference.

I found the Internet. I realized that "instructional design" wasn't just a random term, but actually had a whole field behind it—books, degree programs, professors, theories, and terminology. I bought books about e-learning including *E-Learning and the Science of Instruction* by Ruth Clark and Richard Mayer and *Michael Allen's Guide to E-Learning*. I discovered that people were blogging about e-learning and instructional design, and in 2006, I started blogging and connecting with these very people. One of my first blog posts was about this company called Kineo, which shared great guides and tips about e-learning and instructional design. If you read my bio you'll know that I ended up working for them a few years later. In 2007, I attended my first eLearning Guild conference and got to hear people like Clark Quinn and Will Thalheimer speak. My world was opening up in a big way.

I started debating with people online as to whether one needed a degree to practice instructional design. "You go to a medical doctor," they would argue. "You hire a licensed architect to build your home. You should also trust your instructional design to professionals who know what they're doing."

To that I simply said, "Pshaw." I had kids and a full-time job, and the truth was, I didn't have time to go back to school. I figured—and have hopefully proven—that although I'm an instructional designer by accident, that doesn't mean I don't know what I'm doing or that I can't learn.

Thus—10 years into my career of designing CBTs and e-learning programs—I began my informal effort to teach myself a thing or two about instructional design and adult learning theory.

What About You?

What's your story? Was your path to instructional design similar? Did you have your sights set on something quite different than what you've turned into, or is this exactly what you expected for yourself?

When I have this conversation with groups of instructional designers, there's usually a lot of affirming head nods. And some very funny stories.

- "I was working as a bank teller and I was good at what I did, so they asked me to help out with the training classes."

- "I had a knack for formatting PowerPoints—when they needed someone to learn this new authoring tool, they asked me."

- "We were short-staffed and needed someone who could help out."

- "I inherited responsibility for training materials when someone went out on maternity leave."

- "I'm a good writer and it seemed a natural fit."

We find our way here by accident, but that doesn't mean it will turn into a complete disaster. Sometimes it will, but not always.

Accidental ID—My Epiphany

True confession: I stumbled into my instructional design job about 14 years ago. My position was going to be eliminated in a re-org and it was the only way my boss could keep me on staff.

Another confession: I only recently realized that what I was doing was a real thing—a profession even—and that my job could entail more than just collecting information and sharing it through a glorified website.

Sure, I had an "instructional designer" job title and possessed all the necessary skills and competencies listed on my annual performance review, but my job on paper bore little resemblance to my job in reality. Thanks to some certificate workshops I had a good grasp of the theories and mechanics of instructional design, but—at best—most of what I was doing was amateur graphic design with a touch of editing. Need that PowerPoint dressed up? I was your gal! Need that introduction to be rewritten? Look no further!

And then it happened. In the summer of 2007 I opened an email from a fellow designer, which had a link to a post on Tom Kuhlmann's "The Rapid eLearning Blog." The post was about getting more from subject matter experts—but the ideas were not only relevant, they were also revelatory. As I read through the blog's archives, I realized that Tom was putting words to the ideas that had bubbled around my head for years. Maybe my job could be more than just reorganizing whatever piles of paper the SME gave me. Maybe I didn't have to push loads of boring, static content at people. Maybe my job could be more than just a PowerPoint monkey. Maybe I could actually make the kind of training that people wouldn't mind taking AND that achieved all those objectives I was always rewriting.

Almost more gratifying than Tom's words was reading the comments from fellow readers. Week after week I devoured each post, eagerly scrolling down to take in all the comments and ideas being shared. Reading Tom's blog made me realize for the first time that I wasn't alone! There were hundreds of people all thinking the same things, struggling with the same challenges, and grappling with the same realization: I can design with intent.

Design, by virtue of nearly any definition, is about intent—in our case instructional intent. But how do you move your design from being competent to compelling? My epiphany was when I realized that my job was to make things compelling. And even if my job was accidental, I didn't have to be. I realized that I could do some pretty gratifying work by allowing myself to move from passive design to passionate design.

—Trina Rimmer, Chief Designer, Rimmer Creative Group

From Classroom Trainer to E-Learning Instructional Designer

I started my career training users of a computer-aided design software. I spent the majority of my time in front of the class, teaching material generated by other people, so I never gave much thought to how it was created. Eventually my company asked me to help develop a course that had been written by an office in Germany. I followed the structure of the material that was already there and simply translated the material to English. While I wasn't concerning myself with any instructional design, that project made me realize that I enjoyed the aspect of creating classroom material.

After leaving that position I signed on with a company that was developing material from scratch for the same software. Because I had a lot of experience with the material from the previous company, I followed that model to create the new material. I still wasn't thinking about design principals, I was merely following past experiences. Eventually, I was hired as the internal training developer for another company that used the same design software. Around this time I also started working on an MBA, but soon realized it was not for me.

I became aware of programs that offered a master's degree in instructional design or instructional technology. As I started looking into these degree programs, I realized there was a whole world of instructional design out there. In the past, the design was always done for me and I just followed the model. Now, many of the Internet resources I found showed me what good instructional design was.

Around the same time, I was also introduced to the world of e-learning, when I was asked to make an online course. I quickly realized there was a way things should be done to create good content. I never did pursue one of those master's programs as I realized that the web had many resources that I could use to learn about instructional design. Now, almost 10 years later, I still use a lot of those resources and continue to learn how to effectively design and implement content.

—Sean Putnam, Director of Training and Documentation,
Altair Engineering

Finding a Passion for E-Learning, by Accident!

After leaving high school I was really unsure what I wanted to do or where I wanted to focus my studies, so I began pursuing subjects that were of most interest to me prior to post-secondary education. That led me to a mix of computer science, biology, and accounting. I worked in accounting departments at several companies and after a few years I found myself wanting a different kind employment. As something to hold me over until I found the "right" position, I got a job at the local hospital as a clerk in the ICU. Shortly after that, an administration position opened within the hospital in the organization development department.

For a few years I worked as the admin support until my then manager presented me with the opportunity become a facilitator for a certain tool we were using. This motivated me to get a better understanding of how my manager and co-workers went about doing their jobs as the organization's trainers, facilitators, and cultural development.

I started taking online courses in adult education and training. After finishing these courses, my passion for e-learning was firmly in place and I wanted to find out how to create and develop e-learning programs. I began pursuing course after course and certificate after certificate. If there was a free webinar I could tap into, I did. If there was a blog I could follow, I would sign up and add it to my feed.

We trialed a few different systems in the early 2000s, but it wasn't until 2007 that we finally brought our current learning management system. Because I had the right background, I was charged with overseeing the full implementation and administration of the system. My training also gave me the opportunity to design and develop almost all of the system's content. Since beginning my "career journey" I have never stopped learning, exploring, and developing new skills to continue my pursuit of developing and delivering the best content or solutions for our learners.

—Tracy Hamilton Parish, Education Technology
Specialist at a Regional Healthcare Center

What I Do Today

As I write this, I have been doing the instructional design thing for nearly 17 years. I've been an integral part of the design team for hundreds of self-paced online training programs. Hundreds. From software training to soft skills for banks, supermarkets, hair care companies, insurance agencies, entertainment companies, global nonprofits, oil and gas, retail chains, you name it. Some of these programs have won awards, but others have been complete training wrecks.

Most of the learning experiences I create are self-paced online learning programs—people sit down in front of a computer and go through them on their own, either in a matter of minutes or hours. I also help with more blended learning designs, which means looking beyond the self-paced experience to incorporate face-to-face classroom sessions, instructor-led online classrooms, mobile performance support and job aids, refresher trainings, and so on. But my main bread and butter is still designing self-paced online learning for the corporate market.

Since joining the field in 1996, I have always worked on the supplier side—for companies whose sole purpose in life was to create learning programs for other companies. This means that I can specialize and focus on what I do well. I work with clients to understand needs and requirements. I design the learning experience, write scripts, and work with production teams who have expertise in technology and graphics. In the past I have acted as my own project manager, but recently I have had the luxury of having someone else—with project management expertise—do that task.

I like to think that my job is to help other people do their jobs better. Whether they're for bank tellers, hair stylists, or middle managers learning to lead teams for the first times, the training and resources I design help people better serve their customers and their employees.

If I can help someone do his job better, perhaps I really can help make the world a better place. This could be my hippie idealism shining through my corporate learning façade, but I think there's truth to the notion that those of us involved with corporate training are helping people. At least, I hope we are.

Why Accidents Will Keep Happening

As technology-based learning continues to slip into the mainstream, we'll see accidents—in the form of accidental instructional designers—happening more and more. Companies will continue to scramble to find ways to deliver information and tools to the masses. The need for training will continue to spring up organically, like mushrooms on a soggy lawn. Start-up companies will need to train their employees on how to manage their fledgling teams. Organizations will create new products that customers will want to learn how to use. Legal requirements will mandate that employees learn the rules and demonstrate compliance with regulations. Businesses will want to teach skills to improve sales or manage a new technology. And of course, people will want to help their employees actually do their jobs better.

And because we've all been trained to think that training is always the solution and that just about anyone can figure out how to do it, we will find people to create that training. Within businesses and organizations, managers and leaders will continue to tap heads to turn regular people, who know the content or show some talent at crafting a PowerPoint deck, into instructional designer and trainers. Here are just a few ways that can happen.

Tap! A content expert is magically anointed with new superhero ID powers! Armed with his new e-learning authoring tool, he can now dump all of that precious, tacit knowledge from his head into an online self-study program. "Look, Ma, I created a 342-slide PowerPoint deck and can publish it to our learning management system to prove that everyone has learned!"

Tap! That certain someone who acts most like that well-loved kindergarten teacher from 1973 now leads the organization's classroom training sessions! She has the personality and the charisma and makes training F-U-N!

Tap! That new employee who says she took a graphics class in school can figure out this technology stuff. Let's give her an authoring tool and she can create pretty courses.

And many other examples like those will continue to happen—and that's OK. Small organizations with small budgets may not have the ability to hire chief learning officers and take formal approaches to building training teams. Instead they figure out the best way to help people do their jobs better with the resources they have.

To the uninitiated and the naïve, it does seem like anyone can be an instructional designer. Advancements in technology have created easy-to-use e-learning authoring tools and templates, so now anyone can create "instruction." It's a beautiful and terrifying world. But that's the reality, so let's live with it, forge a path forward, and find some intentional ways of doing what we do.

About This Book

This book is filled with tales and tips from my experience and perspective. I'll share techniques and strategies I've picked up over the years while working with subject matter experts from all walks of life, writing countless design documents and storyboards/scripts, and reviewing and testing courses until my eyes bled. I won't be talking too much about specific technologies or teaching you how to use any of the tools.

In part I, I'll take a look at the big picture: What is instructional design? What is design? And why does design even matter?

In part II, I'll take you on more of a practical journey, looking at simple things you can start doing today to create learning programs that more effectively engage fellow humans. Each chapter has a particular focus, although there may be some overlap as I explore the same areas from different angles.

In part III, I'll send you off into the wide world of instructional design with yet more ideas for turning your practice from an accidental to an intentional one.

Much of this information is geared toward the new practitioner—the recent accident. I hope this book serves as a jumping off point for you as you find your own unique passion in what you do and seek to do it even better. For readers with more experience, there may be some new tidbits in here, as well as some familiar ideas that you're happy to reconnect with.

Throughout the book I've sprinkled resources and ideas for further reading—what I read late at night as I continue to hone my skills. I hope you'll find some ideas and inspiration for taking your own discovery and personal learning journey to the next level.

I assume you're reading this book because you want to and I hope that your journey from accident to intention is one that you're willing to share with me. I really think we can get better at what we do each and every day.

part I

chapter 1

On Instructional Design and E-Learning Pie

In this chapter . . .

- What is instructional design?

- How many ways can you spell ID?

- What four areas do you need to understand in order to be a well-rounded e-learning professional? (Hint: there's pie involved!)

As instructional designers, most of us have a hard time describing what we do to the rest of the world. Instructional designer is not a job title that resonates even mildly with most people. So how can we describe our work more accurately? Looking at textbook definitions of instructional design may not help with your next cocktail party conversation about your work, but they may provide a starting point.

In a volume of essays that is lovingly referred to by those who actually went to school for ID as "The Big Green Book," Charles Reigeluth, a professor in the instructional systems technology department at Indiana University, defined the discipline of instructional design as being "concerned primarily with prescribing *optimal* methods of instruction to bring about desired *changes* in student knowledge and skills" (Reigeluth, 1983, 4).

Reigeluth talks about the distinction between theories of instructional design, which focus on methods of instruction and what a teacher does, as opposed to theories of learning, which focus on the learning process itself. As someone involved with designing instruction, it makes sense to know more both about how people learn and what methods work to help them learn more effectively.

M. David Merrill is an instructional effectiveness consultant, professor emeritus at Utah State University, and noted academic in instructional design. He makes a distinction between *instructional science* and *instructional design*. In his view, instructional science is the discovery and testing of instructional strategies, whereas instructional design uses those instructional strategies to invent "instructional design procedures and tools that will promote student learning" (Merrill, Drake et al., 1996, 5-7).

This all sounds very well and good for academics, but once you mix technology into the equation and start talking about real people making a living as instructional designers, these definitions get somewhat lost.

In "In Search of the Secret Handshakes of ID," a snappy article in *The Journal of Applied Instructional Design*, Ellen Wagner talks about the ongoing challenge with which those of us who work at the "intersection of learning and technology" have struggled. She notes that there's a lot of fluidity and overlap between terms like *instructional design, instructional technology*, and *educational technology*.

Wagner, a tenured professor of ID, says she

> strove to make the linkages between theory and practice, process and product clear and easy to understand for my students and in my work products. I ensured that my students were exposed to the theoretical underpinnings of learning, cognition, and instruction. I made sure they understood that media selection was contingent upon the analysis of the learner, the learning, and the conditions of learning. I considered definitions as noted in the previous paragraphs as robust, defensible, researchable aspects of the discipline. And then I left the academy. (Wagner, 2011)

What happens once you leave the academy of instructional design? You discover that the real world defines instructional design in a myriad of ways.

In practice, *instructional designer* is an umbrella term that covers a whole slew of people and jobs. Chances are, if you walked into a room filled with people who call themselves instructional designers, they would all have a slightly different definition of what they do and how they do it. One designer might say he builds courses using Articulate Storyline, while another says she does needs analysis and maps content to instructional strategies. A third might say she lays out content on a page, and another says he's focused on creating lesson plans for live classrooms.

In 2010, I had the privilege to present at an e-learning conference with Ellen Wagner and Koreen Olbrish Pagano. We called our session "New Skills for Instructional Designers," and as part of the prep work we looked at what the ID schools say they teach versus what companies actually want to hire.

The results were eye-opening.

The school descriptions included lofty terms like "learning," "theory," and "assessment." Businesses trying to hire instructional designers, on the other hand, were asking for a large variety of job skills all lumped under the ID category. The following is a list I recently pulled from actual job listings for instructional designers. The job descriptions included things like:

- needs analysis
- task assessment
- writing learning objectives
- project management
- supplier management
- desktop publishing
- graphic design
- specific knowledge of specific authoring tools including Articulate Presenter, Captivate, and Lectora
- PowerPoint
- conduct live and recorded webinars
- support the training database
- knows ADDIE process
- experience working with SMEs
- experience creating ILT, facilitator's guide, or student guides.

The story these job listings tell reinforces at least two things for me:

1. There is a disconnect between what a lot of ID programs teach their students and what industry needs. I don't mean to disrespect all ID programs in a wholesale manner. In fact, I know of quite a few that are well-grounded in practical application and seem to produce graduates who can produce the type and quality of work product that Corporate America is looking for.

2. There really are many, many shades of instructional design.

A Matter of Degrees

A fun conversation that I like to get into with academic types who teach instructional design, or have degrees in instructional design, is the age old debate of "degree" or "no degree." When I find myself debating with those who say, "You need a degree in instructional design in order to do it right," I don't completely disagree with them. There is a lot of value in getting a degree in ID or educational technology—you learn core concepts and theories and (hopefully) practical application.

Deciding to go back to school in instructional design is a personal choice and a path you may choose to go down for all the right reasons. A degree or certificate may be just the thing if you're looking to break into this field or want to take your skills to the next level. It might give you the structure and foundation that you need. At the *advanced* stage of my career, I personally do not see a need to get a degree in ID. If I had the time and the money, I might look into something like cognitive science. But I'm completely cool with where I'm at, mostly because I have made a concerted effort to learn more on my own. But I don't think it's realistic to demand or expect that everyone who does what we do has a degree and I don't think it will ever happen.

What's the reality out in the field? I've been running an informal survey on my blog for the last five or so years. I asked, "If you work as an instructional designer, do you have a degree in instructional design?"

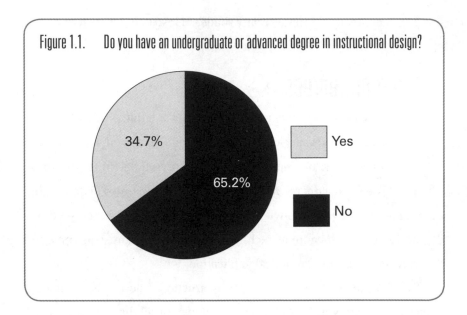

Figure 1.1.   Do you have an undergraduate or advanced degree in instructional design?

34.7%

65.2%

Yes

No

As of February 15, 2014, 65 percent of more than 650 respondents report that they do not have an advanced degree in instructional design. This has held strong for a couple years, so I'm willing to say that it's a good representation of what's actually happening. And the degrees that people do have were interesting, too: marine biology, literature, political science, English, chemistry, anthropology, French, geoscience, and home science. It's really quite a list. When I asked, "If you do not have a degree in instructional design, have you ever been denied work because of that lack?" The overwhelming response was "no" (83 percent).

So where do we start from and what do those of us who end up doing this work aspire to be? A couple of years ago I ran another informal survey asking practicing instructional designers what they wanted to be when they grew up. The answers were both enlightening and entertaining:

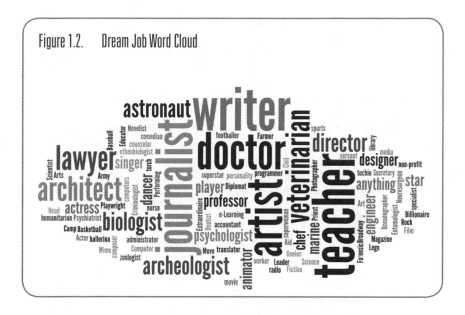

Figure 1.2. Dream Job Word Cloud

It looks like those of us who end up in this field have an interest in education and writing, a curiosity to understand things more deeply, and a desire to help people. (And, of course, a passion for saving the world and demonstrating superpowers.) There's also a smattering of interest in things technical, which may be more of a sign of the times in which some of us grew up.

That's what we all thought we wanted to be. But what do we actually do? If you survey people who identify themselves as practicing instructional designers, you'll find a lot of variation in their job descriptions. Some instructional designers:

- Conduct thorough needs analyses of organizations to evaluate what the right solution for a problem might be.
- Write storyboards and scripts for self-paced e-learning programs.
- Develop and author e-learning programs using an off-the-shelf authoring tool.
- Create complex simulations and games using Adobe Flash.

- Work with 3D immersive role playing tools like Second Life.

- Use web 2.0 technologies to design collaborative, just-in-time training experiences.

- Look at organizations' structures and define strategy.

- Craft distance learning events for college credit that pull together elements of both asynchronous and synchronous learning experiences.

- Create online learning experiences for use in K–12 classrooms.

- Manage online learning communities and curate content.

In a 2009 blog post, "The Various Roles of Instructional Design," Jonathan Atleson broke ID down into the specific shades and gave them names, including:

- instructional designer

- instructional systems designer

- instructional (multimedia) developer

- instructional technologist

- instructional systems developer

- instructional systems analyst

- trainer/training specialist

- e-learning/multimedia project manager.

I'd add a few instructional design–related job titles I've noticed in the last few years (as well as some I've been called):

- learning designer

- interactive designer

- script writer

- e-learning developer.

That's quite a list with quite a few different roles and some rather varied skill sets.

Is it a problem that everyone seems to have their own definition of instructional design? Or that there are numerous shades of ID? What do you think?

The E-Learning Pie

Why do so many different skills get lumped under one basic job title? It really speaks to the complexity of the discipline that is online learning in the corporate world. To dive more deeply into this, let's talk about pie. E-learning pie, that is.

While preparing for our "New Skills for Instructional Designers" session, Ellen Wagner turned me on to her schema for the e-learning profession. She said that well-rounded, e-learning professionals need to be versant in some very different areas if they're going to be successful in this business. There are four slices in a big pie, with each piece representing a critical part of the profession: learning, creativity, technology, and business.

1. Learning

The first piece is all about learning and pedagogy/andragogy: how we learn and how we assess whether or not people have learned. It's adult learning theory, instructional design, learning objectives, and behavioral and performance change. These are the teachers, instructional designers, and people who get very excited about assessments. They think about how to help people learn better and want to understand how humans think, act, and behave.

2. Creativity

Next is the creative slice. These are the writers, graphic artists, video producers, film directors, and game designers (although game designers could also fit into the learning section. Yes, there's overlap). These people make beautiful e-learning material that pulls you in. They tell compelling stories that make people want to stick around and learn.

The truth is, without creative talent in e-learning, we might just end up with lists of really boring learning objectives.

3. Technology

The third piece is technology. Electronic media is what put the "e" in e-learning after all. Where would we be without the programmers, developers, builders, authoring tool users, LMS creators, and people who know about SCORM and data analytics? Technology pulls it all together, and without it, well, it's not technology-based learning, is it?

Not all designers are technicians, but you need to know what you're working with and how far you can take it. You at least need to speak the language, understand the terms, and know when you're in over your head and need to contact an expert.

4. Business

Whether you're in academia or on the corporate side of the industry, there's always the business piece of the pie to consider. This is where you need to understand business needs, strategic goals and vision, consultancy, ROI and measurement, project management, and client management. Understanding the business piece ensures that you're delivering a commercially sound project that meets your business needs, is on time, and on budget.

The Whole Pie

Ever felt a little schizophrenic as an instructional designer? Now you have a reason. These four slices of pie represent different skill sets and interests. However, each one is integral to a successful e-learning initiative; failure to focus on one of these pieces may cause your program to fall flat.

E-Learning Pie: Know Your Strengths!

Learning, Pedagogy, and Assessment

- ☐ Adult learning theory
- ☐ Behavior change
- ☐ Instructional strategies
- ☐ Assessment
- ☐ Curriculum design
- ☐ Learning objectives

Creativity

- ☐ Facilitation and performance (for live instruction)
- ☐ Writing (copy writing, script writing)
- ☐ Video production
- ☐ Audio
- ☐ Visual design
- ☐ User experience design
- ☐ Game design
- ☐ Animation
- ☐ Storytelling

Technology

- ☐ Authoring tools
- ☐ Programming (.net, Java, PHP, CSS, HTML)
- ☐ SCORM/AICC/xAPI
- ☐ Learning management systems
- ☐ Quality assurance and testing
- ☐ Tracking and reporting

Business

- ☐ Business needs assessment
- ☐ Conducting focus groups
- ☐ Data analysis
- ☐ ROI
- ☐ Consulting skills
- ☐ Project management

The E-Learning Pie in Practice

I feel pretty lucky that my e-learning career has always been on the supplier side of the business, working for companies that design and develop e-learning for other companies. Because we're the experts, we have dedicated people who focus on what they're uniquely good at: graphic artists who design beautiful layouts; instructional designers who do needs analysis and define learning objectives; salespeople and account managers who map it all back to the organization's business needs; writers who pull off the perfect scripts; project managers who make it all run like clockwork—on time and on budget; developers who know the tools, speak the SCORM, and take care of the things that make me want to stick my fingers in my ears and sing "la la la."

Those of you who work as a one-person e-learning shop, either on your own as a freelancer or within an organization, have a bit of a challenge—somehow you need to represent all of these pie slices. If you can do that all really well, you're some kind of superhero. If not, then you may be falling flat in some way or you're getting help from outside your organization to fill in your gaps.

The truth is, a lot of e-learning projects just represent a few parts of the pie. Have you ever seen an e-learning program that's full of learning and technology, but nothing else? It's instructionally sound and filled with learning objectives that begin with all the proper verbs. It makes great use of technology that brilliantly passes seat time and final test results back to the learning management system. But, man-o-man, is it boring. And so the initiative fails because it's missing the creative touch and a clear connection back to the business objectives.

Some projects might just showcase the creative and technology pieces of the pie and try to pass it off as e-learning—but then it's something else entirely. Some might call it pure entertainment.

The most successful e-learning initiatives pull all these pieces together: they have a clear vision of what the audience needs to learn and how to best achieve that outcome; a creative design that looks enticing, creates interest, and sustains attention; the right technology that stands up to the delivery needs; and a solid connection back to the overall goals and objectives of the organization.

But that kind of project is typically the work of a well-balanced team. Because, frankly, that's a lot of hats for one person to wear.

T-Shaped Skills

So is your job to get deep expertise in all pieces of the e-learning pie? Maybe. But let's take a look at another model, in the shape of the letter T.

The e-learning field is a knowledge-based profession that really fits a T-shaped skills model. We need broad skills and understanding (the top of the T), with potentially one area of deep expertise (the vertical bar of the T). The horizontal bar enables you to communicate and collaborate with experts across a wide range of disciplines, making you a versatile generalist with a well-rounded pointed of view. The deep vertical bar makes you a specialist.

Scott Abel, in a post on content strategy, "Content Strategists Must Become Engineers of Content-Driven Customer Experiences," writes of this specialist versus generalist theme:

> It's also clear that while specialists exist in every field, you wouldn't expect a general practitioner (a medical doctor who is trained to provide primary healthcare to patients of either sex and any age) to say she doesn't know anything about how to treat the infection on your foot because she's not a podiatrist (doctor who specializes in foot care) or a dermatologist (doctor who specializes in skin care). Sure, she may need to refer you to one of these specialists should your problem be difficult to cure, or extremely unusual. But, because all physicians have a common understanding of how the body works, a general practitioner could be expected to have sufficient knowledge to talk to you intelligently about the infection, and offer imme-diate treatment (if warranted). Of course, if she found that her education and experience did not prepare her to help you overcome your medical challenge, as a professional, she would seek guidance from a specialist.

Know Your Sweet Spot, Know Your Weakness

What is your favorite piece of pie? What is your sweet spot? What pulled you into this field? For me, it was writing and teaching. Although I didn't get an education degree, I apparently had an inclination to teach. I've also found that I have the ability to communicate ideas and processes to people in a way that makes sense.

My agnostic area has always been the technology side. I don't speak code, I don't understand variables, I cringe when someone wants to talk SCORM. I know enough to know when I need to pull in a specialist, and that's what really matters.

If you're happy with your part of the pie, focus on that craft and hone your skills. Become a specialist and make that your vertical, but be sure to keep your eye on the broad skills and all four pieces of the pie. However, if you have the bigger picture in mind, then take the time to learn what you need to about the other pieces. Just don't spread yourself too thin or you could get watered down. We can't be experts in everything and with technology changing so quickly, there's a lot to keep track of, like alternative reality games, virtual worlds, mobile technology, rapid e-learning, SCORM, xAPI, graphics, instructional design, authoring tools, social media, big data, 3D printing, augmented reality, and HTML5. It's enough to make your head spin. Mine sure does.

Make an effort to build a community and network to help you and round out your pie. Today it is so easy to connect with people and resources to learn from and share their expertise. You can use Twitter to find people who know more about the business of e-learning than you, hone your creative craft by reading blogs about writing or video production, read books about instructional design strategies, and talk to professors who know the research about what makes adults pay attention. Go to technology-based learning conferences and find your people—hear firsthand what other organizations are doing and how they are creatively solving their problems.

Even if you are working as a one-person shop in your organization, you are not alone. In the next building, across town, and around the world, there are thousands of people figuring out how to deliver better learning solutions using technology. You are not alone and your problems are not unique. We are all here to help.

chapter 2

Why Design Matters

In this chapter . . .

- Huddle around the campfire for the thrilling and horrifying tale of . . . the CBT Lady!

- Who gets to call themselves a designer?

- What is design and why does it matter to e-learning?

- What are the hallmarks of good design and how can we incorporate those into e-learning?

A Cautionary Tale

Once upon a time, I went winter camping with my son's youth group. (OK, so we stayed in a cabin with a wood stove and had access to plumbing and a fully electric kitchen, but still—winter camping, right?) There I was, the lone mom with 14 boys and their dads, when the inevitable question came up: "What do you do for work?"

Explaining my work has always been hard to do. After years of receiving blank stares or weak smiles to the response, "I design e-learning programs," I've found different things to say. Depending on the audience, I may say something lame like, "I write" or "I do training stuff," which could be enough to get a nod of recognition. If I think the person might have ever taken an e-learning program, I say, "I create online learning programs for companies—you know, like distance learning." As the years have gone by and online learning has gone more mainstream, this conversation has gotten easier. Although I can't say that I've become more eloquent in my delivery.

But I was not prepared for the response I got this time. When I gave my line about how I design the corporate training programs that people take on their computers, one of the dads started hissing at me. He actually formed his two index fingers into the shape of a cross and hissed at me. "You're the CBT Lady," he cried out in complete horror.

He went on to describe the true suffering he had endured while being forced to complete hour after endless hour of boring, locked down e-learning programs. "The CBT Lady! You make those awful presentations that just read out every single word that's written on the screen. And I can't click to move on to the next page until it's all over. And then I have to take a 20-question quiz and I get to the end of the quiz and I have to take the whole thing over again because I got one question wrong!"

"I try to do it better than that! That's not what I'm about!" I protested, attempting to defend myself and my profession. My words fell on deaf ears. This man had suffered and would hear nothing more.

Weeks later he introduced me to his wife: "Honey, she's the CBT Lady!"

His wife works in the pharmaceutical industry and had similar tales of woe and suffering. Lucky for her, she was a manager and mostly only had to tell her employees to complete the required e-learning programs. I guess you could say management does have its perks.

So now I can't help but picture cranky CBT ladies locked in closets at organizations all over the country, wearing hair nets like tired lunch ladies from a junior high school cafeteria slopping food onto plates. Hunched over their laptop computers, they listlessly convert boring PowerPoint decks into even more boring e-learning programs. "It ain't glamorous," they say, "but it's a living."

I'll go out on a limb and say that for the first seven or eight years of my career I was the CBT Lady. Sadly, there's probably a little bit of her in all of us. And even if you've done a lot of work to reform your inner CBT Lady, chance are she'll pop out of you every once in a while. "Hey, throw another text bullet or five on that screen. Your SME says all of that content is important, just do it!"

This kind of training is what organizations spend thousands of hours and millions—perhaps billions—of dollars a year creating. According to ASTD's 2013 *State of the Industry* report, U.S. organizations spent $164.2 billion on employee learning and development in 2012, with technology-based delivery of instruction at 39 percent of formal hours. That's a lot of e-learning. And then think of the thousands, perhaps millions, of hours that employees must endure of this awful, awful stuff, so they can tick off a required box in their learning management system and say, "See, I learned it!"

Instead of paying attention to any of it, what are the learners doing? Multitasking? Checking emails while that audio file finishes playing? Using Twitter on their phones as yet another text bullet builds on the screen? Looking at the Dow Jones stock sticker? Taking screen shots of content screens and pasting them into a Word document so they can correctly answer the test questions at the end of the hour?

Have you asked around to find out what people are really doing with your e-learning programs? Have you ever seen if the answers to the final test for that mandatory training course you created are posted on the refrigerator in the lunchroom? Because that happens all the time.

Employees roll their eyes at e-learning. They see it as a chore. What about you? Have you had to take required or mandatory e-learning programs? Did the CBT Lady make them?

The point is, this is what a lot of people think about this profession and the work that e-learning designers and developers put out there in the name of training. Is this what you want your name on? Is this how you want to be known?

Do you know how the people in your organization currently view your formal learning offerings? Is classroom training seen as a punishment for poor performance? Is it a breezy day or two out of the office with free lunch? What about e-learning? Is it simply a required task to be endured while otherwise multitasking?

Before you go out and spend another minute planning your next learning initiative, find out how people perceive what you're already doing. Do they—real people who have to take these courses (and not their managers who say they must, or the subject matter experts or project stakeholders who say why it's important)—find any real value in e-learning? Conduct surveys or get an informal feet-on-the-street view of what's really happening. You may want to walk around and check out the kitchens or break rooms. Are the answers to the latest compliance e-learning assessment circulating on a printed cheat sheet? Ask questions that you may not like the answers to, such as:

- Tell me about that last e-learning program you took. What did you learn?

- Did it help you do your job better?

- What do you remember about it? (The pretty colors? The content? That flashy animation at the end? Or the performance improving tips and advice you received?)

- Have you ever gone back to look at it again?

- Did it provide you with information you needed when you needed it?

- Would you recommend it to a colleague?

- Do you want to take more e-learning programs like this one?

- What would be really to useful to you?

Ask people what they think. If they're really being honest, you might get responses that will take your breath away. More importantly, I hope you get responses that will inform and possibly change your direction in a real and meaningful way.

So what's the CBT Lady's fundamental problem? She just doesn't understand how to put together something more than gloppy mystery meat on a plate. She needs to understand nutrition, and learn how to serve up delicious tasting meals that also look appealing. Instead, she develops courses and converts information. But she doesn't design. Maybe she's just doing her job; maybe she just doesn't care.

But you care, right? Because you're not the CBT Lady.

Who Is a Designer?

When you hear the word *designers*, who do you imagine? What are their jobs? Do they wear hipster glasses and skinny jeans while sipping iced chai lattes? Do they sit at drafting tables making architectural sketches or in front of laptops playing with Illustrator or Photoshop? Depending on who you talk to, *designer* might be synonymous with *graphic designer* or *website designer*.

In a lot of people's minds, design is about the aesthetics or the visual presentation—the way something looks or the way a page is laid out. In recent years, design has taken on a very digital association—there's an assumption that the designer works with computers and designs things for the computer screen. I've seen design books that are clearly geared toward webpage designers, with an emphasis on fonts and color palettes.

When people write about their little design niche they'll often refer to it as "the design profession" or "the design industry." And yet, what they're actually talking about is website design as an industry or industrial design as an industry. Many disciplines across a wide range of industries and areas have designers—there are software designers, theater designers, industrial designers, packaging designers, experience designers, road designers, food designers, floral designers, and sound designers (to name just a few). There is so much more to design, and one field can't lay sole claim on the territory.

So who gets to call themselves a designer? If I were to show up at a fancy design school function and proclaim myself an "instructional designer," would I get laughed at? Or, would I get embraced and welcomed into the fold? If you look at any prestigious design school's website, you won't find instructional design on their list of specialties, you'll see visual design, graphics, fashion, and so on. Trained instructional designers, as you may already know, come from education programs, not design schools.

What Does It Mean to Design?

When you start digging around, it turns out that there really isn't one definition of design. It's kind of a shifting, amorphous thing, depending on who you're talking to. The different definitions get to the heart of the tension between creativity and process.

Design as a Verb vs. Design as a Noun

The New Shorter Oxford English Dictionary dedicates two long entries to the word "design." The first defines design as a noun—in this sense design is:

- a purpose, an intention, an aim

- a plan or scheme; a preliminary sketch or plan from which a building or other work may be made

- an idea as executed, the finished work itself

- the action or art of planning and creating in accordance with appropriate functional or aesthetic criteria.

Thus, the design can be the idea in the architect's head, the blueprints from which the building is built, or the building itself. For any of those, someone might say, "This design looks really good."

The second entry defines design as a verb:

- to plan or execute

- to make drawings or sketches

- to intend, purpose, create.

When an architect designs a building she forms an idea in her head of how it will look, she makes blueprints, and then the builders construct the building.

So, design can either refer to the plan that you come up with, the intention, the process for coming up with that plan, or the thing that you made. That's quite a word, isn't it?

The Difference Between Design and Art

Artists make beautiful things. Designers make beautiful things. Is that the same? Matt Ward, a digital artist and creative director, wrote a great blog post, "What Is Design?," in which he wrote, "Art can exist for art's sake.

Design cannot." The difference is that design must have a purpose. Ward says there are three pillars to design: purpose, intention, and content. When you think about the learning programs that you are designing, consider these three things.

Purpose dictates that every element of the design should contribute to achieving a goal. Why does the learning program need to exist in the first place? What is the reason?

Intention refers to the thoughtful consideration and placement of every element and all the details. It's having a reason for specific choices—from where a button is located, to the size of the font. What is your intention behind each screen and activity? How does it serve your overall purpose? Did you make a choice about fonts and layouts? Intention means that you thoughtfully considered every element, and didn't just go by blind default.

Content functions as the framework—it's the lens through which the design is focused. It is what you're communicating. Why are you including that content? How does it support your purpose or inform your intention? For instance, the content may influence the typeface you choose or the overall look of the program.

Nancy Duarte, author of *slide:ology: The Art and Science of Creating Great Presentations*, reminds us that:

> Design is not solely about making things aesthetically pleasing, although that is part of it. Design, at its core, is about solving problems. And whatever that problem is—from squeezing oranges to running faster to communicating effectively—designers strive to help users solve their dilemma in the most convenient, simple, and elegant way. (2008, 83)

So, what is good design? Forget training. Forget e-learning. Think about the world at large. Close your eyes and imagine something that has been well designed. OK, closing your eyes might be hard to do while you're reading. So consider this well designed thing, and *then* when you have closed your eyes try to experience that thing. Ready? Go.

Now, hold that thing in your mind and consider the following:

- How does it look?

- How does it feel?

- How does it make you feel?

- What can you do with it?

- Do you know what to do with it?

I've reflected a lot on the attributes of good design, and it really boils down to these questions.

How Does It Look?

For many of us, the first element of good design is how something looks, the visual *aesthetics*. When we say something has been well designed, that's often what we're referring to—it has the right curves, lines, and colors.

Do you like the way it looks? Does it have a pleasing pattern or symmetry? Do the colors work well together? Do they excite you or calm you or move you? Think about a common household object like a coffee maker. Let's say you're shopping for a new one and checking out the different models on the shelf. Can you say why you like one design over the other?

Well-designed e-learning programs look good. They please the eye and invite the learner in. They make the person feel like someone actually spent time and energy to create the program, and that, therefore, the content must really matter.

How Does It Feel?

Something that is well designed often has a *tactile* aspect to it. When you touch it (assuming it's something you can touch) it just feels right. My favorite mug's handle fits my hand just right, with a solid heft to it giving me the confidence that my morning coffee won't slip away from me when I need it most.

It's a visceral, almost emotional thing—the weight and balance of an object in your hands, the feeling when you enter a room, the awe-inspiring façade of a building. When we talk about something that is well designed, we are often talking about the tactile experience of that thing.

E-learning programs, while typically an on-screen experience, can evoke a tactile experience. If you design screens that have texture and look touchable, like using crinkled paper and textured backgrounds, it helps make the on-screen world feel more real and immersive.

How Does It Make You Feel?

In addition to the physical aspect of a well-designed thing there is also an *emotional* component. How does this thing make you feel? A sense of serenity and calm? Overwhelming productivity? Sad? Happy? Angry? Does the circus website make you want to buy tickets for your family, or give you nightmares about clowns? Perhaps, more importantly, do you like how it makes you feel? The child protection website might have made you sad, but if it inspired you to donate money then the designer was successful.

For e-learning programs, think about the purpose of the program and approach the content with that in mind. How do you want people to feel after completing your program and what you want them to do with that emotion?

Do You Know What to Do With It?

A critical element of design is that you know what to do with this thing. Is it *usable*? Is it intuitive enough that you can figure out what it is and then how you can use it? Or do you need to spend hours reading a manual to figure it out?

Think about a new appliance that you've just taken out of the box. Do you know how to use it or do you need to spend four hours reading the complex instruction manual because you can't figure out which button turns the darn thing on? Have you seen the videos of two-year-olds figuring out an iPad for the first time? They just get it. That's good design.

These days I expect things to be so easy to use that I can just open them up and understand what to do. It may help to have some sense of what the thing can do in the first place, and I may scan the Quick Start manual if there is one, but for the most part I just want to turn the thing on and start using it. If a new app on my phone takes too much effort to figure out, chances are I'm not going to be using it much. And unless I've bought a high-end espresso machine that froths milk and gives me a back massage, I'm just going to expect that my new coffee pot will not need many instructions.

What about your e-learning programs? Is the navigation clear and intuitive or do you need to spend three minutes explaining every button and feature of the interface? Far too often, learning organizations spoon feed people in how to navigate a course, spending precious time explaining where the "next" button is and that they should click it to move on to the next screen. Are people that clueless these days that you need to go through that process? If your program is poorly designed, then maybe. But better yet, take a step back and see how you can simplify things or build that exploration of the interface into the program itself—like great video games do.

Does It Solve a Problem?

The most critical element of design is, does it solve the problem? Does it produce the desired *outcome*? If it's a chair that's supposed to provide good back support, does your back feel supported? Can the corkscrew actually open a bottle of wine or is it better used for shredding corks? As you design an e-learning program, be sure you have clear sight on the actual problem you are trying to solve. Keep that purpose in mind. You might say, "my purpose is to design instruction." Or better yet, "my purpose is to improve performance."

Remember the CBT Lady who created all of that boring e-learning drivel that made people want to gouge their eyes out? What problem is she trying to solve? What is her purpose? To teach people? To tick off a checkbox that compliance regulators can point to and say "yes, this person says they learned this thing"? To bore people? Does she even have a purpose?

Take a step back and look at what you are trying to do within the workplace: improve performance, change behavior, and get people to *do* something differently than before.

As designers of instruction, we need to focus on helping people do their jobs better. Cathy Moore, a well-known e-learning designer and blogger, asks her readers, "Why is so much e-learning so boring? Because we're obsessed with designing information when instead we should be designing experiences. We need to focus on what people need to do, not what they need to know."

As you consider the world around you and the objects and entities within it, consider these five aspects of good design. There could be more, but start with these. Ask yourself if something is well designed. Look at your own work and rate it. Are you lacking in some areas, but better in others?

Each chapter in part II focuses on a different element of design and the design process, helping you connect more closely to your practice as a designer. Let's become more intentional about our practice together.

part II

The E-Learning Design Process

So, we've established by now that you're here completely by accident, right? You had no idea when you were growing up that you wanted to design e-learning programs, but here you are. And now that you're here, you've decided to commit to your practice with great passion and become intentional in your work.

Before we get going, let's talk for a moment about process.

As an instructional designer, you've likely heard about the ADDIE process (analyze, design, develop, implement, and evaluate). If you're new to all of this and not sure what ADDIE is, be sure to read Jane Bozarth's book, *From Analysis to Evaluation: Tools, Tips, and Techniques for Trainers*, which provides a great overview of the process and lot of useful tools and templates.

But, there's nothing special about ADDIE or even anything customized about it that helps you build better "instruction." That's because ADDIE isn't a design model; it's a project management model. It says, "Do these things in this order," while telling you nothing about how to make your project sing and dance and come alive. That's why so many designers, especially those new to ISD, are sort of adrift. ADDIE is a big black box when it comes to the actual design part.

Do a Google image search on "design process" and you'll find a million images, all cleverly labeled, that define a supposedly unique design process for this or that specialty. These glorious processes are all pretty much the exact same steps in the exact same order. And none of them really tell you what to do once you're in that design stage, at least from a creative standpoint.

Whether you follow ADDIE, or take a more agile approach like Michael Allen's Successive Approximation Model (SAM), which has you design, prototype, and review in successive waves and iterations, you're ready to create some better e-learning.

So let's get to work. In part II we will explore some practical tips and strategies that you can begin to apply to your designs. I am primarily thinking about those organizations that are creating, for better or for worse, slide-based e-learning programs using standard, off-the-shelf authoring tools like Articulate Studio, Storyline, Adobe Captivate, Adobe Presenter, and Lectora. There are lots of other tools you can use—from my perspective that part doesn't matter—and I'm not going to teach you how to do a darn thing in any of them. There are a lot of books out there about how to use software tools, but this isn't one of them!

chapter 3

Working With Subject Matter Experts

In this chapter . . .

- How do you explain to your SME what the process is like and what you'll need them to contribute?

- How do you describe your vision of e-learning to your SME and make sure your expectations are aligned?

- What questions should you ask to get the right content and ensure the best outcome?

Meet Mark, a back office expert for a financial services company. With 15 years of industry experience, Mark is the subject matter expert (SME) on your latest e-learning project. He knows this content like the back of his hand—in fact, he wrote the policy. Your job is to get his content into the hands of the employees who need to know what to do with that policy and how it's going to affect their work.

Mark hands you his PowerPoint deck—loads of slides with loads of text. The expectation? That you will turn that deck into a meaningful training experience. Or, at the very least, make sure that every piece of information is magically transported into the brains of each and every individual who is required to sit through it.

Mark loves his content. As an expert, he's invested his career in this subject and he wants everyone to know what he knows. You're new to the company and have never worked with Mark before. You want to create a better e-learning experience—a program that's rich in context and action-able material, with relevant interactivity that ultimately helps people do their jobs better.

Oh, and your deadline is in three weeks!

So, what can you do to maximize Mark's time, guide him in the right direction, and get what you need to meet his goals and your organization's business objectives?

In this chapter, we'll take a look at some key steps you can take as an instructional designer to bring a SME into the process and make sure your visions are aligned. The goal: to make your job easier, his job easier, and to achieve better learning outcomes.

We'll follow Mark in this chapter, but these strategies apply for working with any SME. This is not a step-by-step process; these are some guiding prin-ciples and ideas to apply at all stages of your design and development process.

This chapter is targeted toward the instructional designer who works with a content expert to create e-learning, but a lot of the information could be useful if you're coaching a SME who directly authors e-learning. These tips work for independent consultants and external suppliers who work with their client's content experts, as well as for the in-house designer collaborating with internal content experts.

Thinking Like a Consultant

As a designer of learning, you've created a niche for yourself. You've got expertise. You've read your books and know your research. You have reasons for why you make the design choices that you do, and yet time and time again, you find yourself in the position of simply filling an order.

Mark says, "Make some training material out of this PowerPoint deck."

So, you do. The problem? You turn into the CBT Lady.

You're not a waiter. You're a professional. This requires you to think like a consultant.

A consultant is someone who adds value and doesn't just take orders. She pushes back when necessary, recommends alternate solutions, and sometimes delivers answers that people may not want to hear.

Have a counterargument prepared when Mark says, "Include all these words and make sure they read every single one of them." If he says, "Let's make sure the narrator reads every word aloud," have a statement ready for why you disagree—and a way to handle it. You'll also need to be ready to gently explain to Mark why his approach may not be the best one to take when you present an alternative design approach that is world's away from his initial vision of 30 slides of dense text. You may need to pull out data and research to show him how people really learn and get him thinking less about training and more about performance. Speak with authority. Try using the word "cognitive." Don't be afraid. It's within your scope.

When you learn to work with subject matter experts like Mark, you're focusing on the business piece of your e-learning pie. In this case, you need to be thinking about communication skills, strategic thinking, and general consulting superpowers.

So What Do Good Consultants Do?

Analyze the problem and recommend solutions. Consultants don't just say, "Absolutely, let me turn that deck into e-learning material." They dive into the situation, they ask hard questions, and they get to the root of the problem. Sometimes the answer may not be training.

Educate and provide an alternate viewpoint. Consultants have expertise and can push back. If the stakeholders or SMEs on your project have a bad idea, you can politely tell them why it won't work. It helps if you have research and data to back you up.

Stay current with industry trends and issues. This means two things: know what's going on in the technology-based learning world and know what matters to your company.

Understand the business goals and objectives of your organization. If the solution you help Mark create supports the company's bottom line and ultimately affects what matters to people like your CEO, then you'll have done your job well and made Mark look like a hero.

Hone your communication skills. You need to be a good communicator, in written and verbal communication, which could require practice. To convince Mark to accept your ideas you may need to argue with him. It's not about force-feeding him your ideas, but about educating him and helping him to see learning in a different light.

So what else can you do to make sure you and Mark deliver a really solid program that makes a difference? Let's break it down.

Kick It Off Right

When you start the project with Mark, be sure to kick things off right. Schedule some time to sit down, roll up your sleeves, and plan things out. Think project initiation first, and then content workshop. You could do this in one meeting or two separate sessions, depending on time constraints and how much content you need to discuss.

Find Out What Matters

What project parameters matter to Mark? Does hitting that January 15th date matter more than anything? Or does quality trump schedule? What about budget? It is important to understand what the project constraints are so that you and Mark share the same vision and can work within that box. You may have to make choices together along the way if your schedule is suddenly jeopardized, due to a lost resource, for example.

Ask Mark, "What does success look like on this project? How will we know that we've hit this one out of the ballpark and scored a home run?" His answers may not be what you expect. Document whatever he says and let his vision of success help drive your vision for the project.

Define the Design and Development Process and the SME's Role in It

Although Mark has taken plenty of e-learning programs at your organization, he has never helped create one. He thinks he can hand you the slide deck he presented to senior management a few weeks ago and that you can magically turn that into e-learning material.

Having done this before, you know it's not that easy. Before doing anything else, you need to spend some time with Mark to help him better understand the design and development process, what you're going to need from him, and how long it will take. Spending this time up front to lay out expectations, agree to tasks, and plan a schedule that you can all stick to is the key to staying on time, on budget, and to creating a successful training outcome.

In your project initiation meeting, take the time to really explain the proccss you're going to follow. How are you—as a team—going to do what you need to do? Who's going to do what? Give Mark a high-level description of each of the key project milestones, share some suggested review times for each stage, and get him to start thinking about what he needs to do.

At Kineo, we always walk our client project teams through a Working Together Guide. It describes the overall process we're going to follow, introduces key deliverables, and sets expectations for how much review time and involvement we'll need from them at each stage of the process. We share a graphic flow chart of the process that we talk them through so they can see how things fit together. And, of course, we explain that the process is alive: We can flex and modify if we need to adjust our ways of working.

The goal isn't to scare the pants off Mark and make him run down the halls screaming, but rather to set clear expectations about what's going to happen. He needs to know what to do and how long it's going to take. And you want him to come away from this project looking like a hero.

Agree to Your Schedule

As you walk Mark through the process, be sure to clearly define who is going to do what and by when. Check availability and timelines and set realistic deadlines. In an ideal world, you have a project manager whose job it is to stay on top of these things, but even if you are so lucky, you still need to stay connected with Mark.

In our digital world, it's very easy to fall back on email, track changes, and chat messages to communicate project details and share feedback. This is all well and good and certainly a key part of a smooth project, but make sure to emphasize the importance of face-to-face meetings and detailed content reviews. I've found that the best projects are the ones where we sit down—at least initially—and establish a human connection, build a rapport, and develop a shared understanding. At the very least, make sure the kickoff meeting is face-to-face, ideally in person, and then run virtual meetings for future sessions.

If you're working with a distributed team in multiple locations, you may want to use collaborative tools, screen sharing programs, and online meeting spaces. When I can't meet with a SME in person for the kickoff, I love meeting them using video conferencing. Take time to establish that face-to-face connection. It's a great way to build an early rapport and a sense of connection that goes beyond email.

Make the Deliverables Visual

I've worked with a lot of content experts like Mark. And things don't always work out the way you hope they will.

Imagine this scene: Mark sends you a big fat PowerPoint deck, you write up a design document, and then a script/storyboard. Along the way, there's a lot of back and forth and a lot of edits.

Finally, you deliver an initial working build of the e-learning program (some might call this an alpha). At this point, Mark says, "Oh, so this is how it's going to look. I didn't know."

And then what happens? More edits. Even though you had a signed-off script. The project ends up coming in two months late and, well, we all know time equals money.

So what went wrong? Did Mark change his mind? Does Mark have no regard for budget and timeline? Does Mark just want to make your life extremely difficult? Are you just a terrible designer?

Although the answer to this question may be all of the above, there's more to it than that.

Remember that while Mark has used a lot of e-learning programs, he hasn't had the pleasure of taking any of the programs that you've designed. Frankly, he's used to the work of the CBT Lady and doesn't really understand what you're trying to do. Plus, all he's seen from you so far are documents and PowerPoint decks.

Mark needs to visualize what you're going for. You can help by providing lots of examples of deliverables and the final product early in the design process. Show him examples of similar e-learning projects and samples of the documents that you want him to review along the way. Helping Mark see how you're going to work with his inputs will (hopefully) help him provide you with the right material.

I like to show SMEs a similar piece of e-learning (if one exists) and a sample script. Take a few minutes to show Mark how a sample script maps back to the sample e-learning program. Are there screen types that you'll be using in this program that you can show him? Any sample interactions? Share as much as you can so he will be able to understand the connection between the early documents and deliverables to your final e-learning product.

An early prototype and working version of your program is an even more effective way to help the SME visualize the end result. We have an ongoing debate within our production team about whether we should skip the script/storyboard phase and just go right to a working version of the course from an early design treatment. We'd still write scripts for our own production process, but we wouldn't have the client go through two or three review cycles when they are likely to change a lot of content later on in the process anyway. I like my scripts so I haven't been convinced this step should be skipped, but maybe I'm just old-fashioned. You might think this makes perfect sense.

Michael Allen advocates an agile method of design, which involves early prototyping. A step away from ADDIE (analyze, design, develop, implement, evaluate), which is essentially a step-by-step sequence with no room for iterations, Allen has moved to SAM (successive approximation model). In the SAM methodology, you start prototyping in the first design workshop meeting.

PowerPoint can serve you well as a rough-and-ready prototyping tool. So can paper and pencils and sticky notes. Prototypes can be back of the napkin, sketches that communicate an idea, a concept, or a flow. The point is to help people visualize sooner rather than later.

Whatever process you follow, make sure that Mark understands what you're aiming for and has a picture in his mind of where you're going. Far too often, I've heard SMEs say, "Well, I just need to see it when we get to alpha to really know what you're trying to do here."

Share Your Design Philosophy

To help Mark visualize the final e-learning product, don't just share sample deliverables and output. Make sure you also share your design philosophy. Talk to him about the CBT Lady—perhaps he's already familiar with her work. Explain to him that you're trying to do something better than that—something that people won't dread having to sit through and that will actually help them do their jobs better.

Share some learning tips and what you aim to do here. Don't forget that you sit in the subject matter expert's seat! Mark is a novice in the area of instructional design, so go gently on him. Some SMEs may not be interested in your ID mumbo jumbo, so don't get too bogged down in explaining theory or dropping technical names. Instead, keep it simple and practical. Explain key concepts, relate it back to Mark's own online experiences, and be sure to provide plenty of examples.

Here are a few key points I like to bring up with SMEs about design.

Remember the Novice

Remind Mark that he is an expert—experts have lots of deep knowledge and typically don't remember what it was like to learn a subject matter for the first time. Subject matter experts, more often than not, want to cram every bit of information they have in their heads into your e-learning program. In their minds, it's all important. They want to magically transpose all the information and knowledge they have spent years accumulating into a 30-minute online program.

As you start asking focused questions regarding content and outcomes, let Mark know that your aim is to create a focused experience that doesn't overwhelm people with too much information. Otherwise, why not just send everyone a PDF with all the information to read at their own leisurely pace? If you can keep him focused on the critical bits, you'll have a stronger, more effective program.

Provide Context

Adding stories to the content will make it more memorable and meaningful to people. Tell Mark that you're going to hit him up for ways to make this content more human and rich through stories.

Chunk the Content

We're often handed huge, dense PowerPoints and expected to absorb it all. However, we know that this isn't an effective way to learn because the human brain can generally only handle three to five new bits of information at once. In *Brain Rules*, John Medina tells us that 10 minutes of focused attention is really as much as the adult brain wants to take in. So, explain the basic principles of "chunking" (short, bite-sized sections of content that can be easily chewed off and digested) to Mark. Try to design a program that can be broken up into 10-minute experiences.

Keep It Short and Sharp

Less really is more. If you're creating a slide-based e-learning program, keep the content focused. A simple screen with text and graphics can be really powerful, but not if you have three paragraphs of text on that screen. Make sure Mark gets this concept so that when you get into script editing mode he's not trying to add hefty blocks of text to your screen designs.

Aim for one idea per slide. It's better to have more slides overall that are shorter and sharper, as opposed to fewer slides that are crammed full of content.

Share Your Approach

At some point during the initial planning phase you may begin developing some ideas about how you think the material should be presented and organized. A knowledge and skill builder or a guided story may come to mind. (See chapter 4 for more on this.) Share your ideas with Mark and tell him why you think they could work. He may have some great ideas that you can build into your design plan.

Sharing your vision for better e-learning materials will hopefully help Mark understand what you are working toward. He can then be involved in making choices about what to include and what not to include. Focusing on what questions to ask Mark during your design process can help with that fine tuning.

Ask the Right Questions

Once you have a shared understanding of process and expectations, you and Mark can take the time to clearly define the desired program objectives. Although Mark provided a thoughtfully prepared 30-slide PowerPoint deck for you to use as "the content," you'll still need to dive deeper, get context, and get to the real crux of the material and what Mark wants people to be able to do after completing the program

This is where a designer's expertise can shine—you know how to ask the right questions to get to that sweet spot in the quickest time possible.

Understand that your time with Mark is probably limited. In fact, he (or any other SME) is probably just squeezing you in between the bits and pieces of his full-time job. Mark's time is precious and potentially critical to the operation on the trading floor. Even a superstar SME who is 100 percent behind your project and totally digs all of the great work your team pushes out, may only have a discrete chunk of time. Be mindful of that and use your time wisely.

So, how can you get the most out of your time?

Before you sit down with Mark to review the content, come up with a list of the key questions you want to ask.

1) **What do you want people to be able to *do*?**

Hopefully this one's a no-brainer and a question you already ask. But it often surprises the subject matter expert. Mark may answer, "We need training on this because we want people to know all the information." Instead, you should try to get him to focus on what people need to do with the information. Does the process change? Do they need to change their behavior? Or is this really just an awareness-raising piece?

At an e-learning conference a few years ago, Ethan Edwards, chief instructional strategist at Allen Interactions, presented on e-learning and the design process. He reminded us that the purpose of e-learning can't be to create expertise, because expertise takes years to develop. Instead, we should be aiming to create minimal competence. So ask Mark, "What's the least that you want people to do?"

What are the three key takeaways that you want someone to get out of this program?

This question helps with prioritization. Get Mark to think about what really matters. If nothing else, what should you absolutely make sure people remember, know how to do, know how to find? I'm often surprised at how few things there really are on this list. And often the SME shares that surprise; "Well, really, I just want them to know who to call if they have a problem identifying the proper risk escalation matrix."

What mistakes do people most commonly make? Where do they get things wrong?

If all you had time for in your program was to focus on the mistakes people make—to prevent them in the future—then you'd make a difference and have fulfilled your purpose in life; or at least proved your worth as an instructional designer.

Ask Mark to think about where things go wrong. If you can put the spotlight on those mistakes—and nothing else—you may have a winner. More importantly, what are the risks and consequences when this gets messed up? Lost sales? Big corporate fines? Loss of your job? What's the risk to the learner and why do they care?

Can you tell me a story about this content? How did you get into this area of expertise? What mistakes have you made along the way?

Be sure to ask questions that get to the heart of the content—this is where the humanity lies. In a classroom session, the sidebar stories—the ones that don't make it onto the instructor's facilitator guide or the PowerPoint deck—are often the bits that make all the difference. Stories add a human element, putting the content into a relevant context that the learner can relate to.

For me, this is always the best part of a content workshop—this is the moment when I can really understand why this e-learning program deserves to exist in the first place. Your challenge, then, is to weave these stories into the program to make the content come alive.

Where should people go for more help and information?

Be sure to ask Mark this last question. Where would he send people if they wanted to learn more? Who would he tell them to call? All those policy documents and detailed PDFs probably exist someplace on the company's intranet. Find out where they live and then point people to those resources in the program.

Next, turn those answers into teaching points, which you'll use to drive your design forward.

When the SME Develops the E-Learning

Not all organizations will work with Mark in the same way we did here. With increasing time pressures and speed to market intensity, designated instructional designers work with a SME's raw content to quickly turn it into an interactive training program—be it self-paced, synchronous e-learning; live classroom; virtual classroom; or some combination thereof. The designer relies on the SME for content expertise, while trying to work within the SME's schedule constraints. After all, the SME also has a full-time day job.

In other organizations, subject matter experts use rapid tools like Articulate Studio to author and develop content on their own, publishing "e-learning" with a few clicks. This has been a revolution of sorts, putting easy-to-use tools in the hands of people with the content know-how. Power to the people, and all that.

However, get a group of trained instructional designers together, typically the ones with the advanced degrees, and quite a debate can arise for and against this tool revolution. The argument for this model is that it saves time and speeds up development. By empowering experts to author the content directly, we can more quickly get the necessary information to our employees so they can do their jobs better.

On the other hand, most SMEs don't know much about adult learning and instructional design. Their expertise revolves around content. With such a narrow focus on the details and intricacies of their content, SMEs typically don't have a sense of the big picture or the expertise to structure content and activities in a meaningful way to teach skills and transfer knowledge. So instead of meaningful training experiences, they create slide after slide of text bullets, uninspired clip art, and a few poorly written multiple choice questions to test "understanding" at the end of the program. Let's face it, the CBT Lady is probably a SME turned instructional designer.

If the latter scenario is what's happening in your organization, see what you can do to help. Your job, should you choose to accept it, is to minimize what Clark Quinn calls instructional design malpractice. Think like a consultant and coach and offer to be a resource or a mentor. This could be seen as a bit disturbing to some of us—the SMEs are taking away my work!—but it will allow you to become more specialized and focused. As you coach and mentor, you hone your expertise and skills even more . . . and you become more indispensable than ever.

Clive Shepherd created a great resource called, "The 60 Minute Masters," which is meant to be a short tutorial on helping subject matter experts get up to speed. Instructional designers will find some good juicy tips in there, too! http://articulate.www.resources.s3-website-us-east-1 .amazonaws.com/products/demos/blog/60-Minute-Masters-no-audio /player.html?noreload=true

chapter 4

What's Your Design Approach?

In this chapter . . .

- How are you going to design a new piece of e-learning? What approach can you take?

- What is a design model?

- What are the three main reasons we design learning experiences?

- Plus a whole bunch of design patterns you can try out!

Let's say you're a new learning designer and someone handed you a Power-Point deck and asked you to turn that into something really good and engaging. He wants it to be interactive and not just the same old boring stuff.

Great. You're excited.

But where do you start? Do you just turn that deck into something slightly more accessible than the original? Do you create a better presentation, or do you attempt to create a meaningful learning experience?

How can you deliver the content in an interesting and engaging way, while providing opportunities for practice and activities to reinforce understanding? Finding the right design approach is about more than throwing spaghetti to a wall to see what sticks. And it's certainly more than just stringing together a bunch of content points from A to Z.

In instructional design lingo, you might say that you need to develop the appropriate instructional strategy in order to best achieve the desired learning objectives. Experienced designers often know what to do somewhat instinctively. Maybe it's because they've already designed 9,042 similar programs? Is it as simple as applying a good heuristic or rule of thumb, like for this kind of learning problem, try this kind of design? Maybe. Maybe not. The risk is that without doing proper analysis you could be missing the real desired outcome and perhaps not designing the right learning solution at all.

Design Models

At Kineo we identify the learning model for a particular e-learning experience early in our design process. The learning model is essentially the design approach you're going to use. According to Matt Fox, director of service delivery at Kineo, "Learning models are patterns of interactions and activities to ensure any learning you create is effective. Using a learning model when developing rapid e-learning allows you to accelerate your writing and development by giving you a repeatable structure to follow."

I've struggled a bit with the terminology over the years as I see similar terms used in similar ways all over the business: learning blueprints, design approaches, instructional methods, and instructional strategies, to name a few. When Mark Harrison and I wrote the article, "Useful Blueprints for Learning Designers," about learning models for Kineo, we went through all the terms and sort of cheated by picking a few of them. Recently, Julie Dirksen, author of *Design for How People Learn*, and Steve Flowers, a performance technologist with the National Archives, turned me on to the concept of design patterns, a term typically used in software and user interface design. A *design pattern* documents some best thinking around solving different types of problems, giving the designer freedom in how to implement the pattern. For instance, software designers might refer to a design pattern that describes an approach for logging into a system or creating an address entry field. The design pattern shouldn't be confused with templates or set screen types. It is not a template or a finished design that can be transformed directly into code, but rather a general description for how to solve a problem.

Whether you call it a learning model or a design pattern or something else, just know that there are a variety of different ways to tackle different problems. There isn't any one specific type of screen you must use or a set look and feel for how you implement it. Instead, it's more of a conceptual approach that you can use as the framework around which to design your program.

By coming up with a set of learning models and developing a shared language around them, you can help your team and your clients better visualize the final e-learning product. You can also point to similar examples of other courses built with that model and explain how they could apply to the content.

Creating Your Objectives

Before we get into any specific models, let's first talk about what you're trying to do. When designing the right learning approach for any topic, you have to be sure about your overall objective. Kineo's Mark Harrison broke it down for me in fairly simple terms, saying there are three main reasons for a learning experience:

- to inform or raise awareness

- to improve knowledge and skills

- to solve complex problems and change attitude or behaviors.

As you begin designing the learning experience, work with your subject matter experts and stakeholders to determine the desired outcomes. My favorite question is, "What do you want the learner to be able to *do* after completing this program?"

Sometimes the answer is really simple, like, "Oh, I really want them to know who to contact if they think their computer has a virus." Or, "I want them to tick off that box in the LMS so we can show that they looked at the information." It's not always straightforward, but it's important to use the right model. This goes back to your initial question: What problem are you trying to solve?

It's all too common to see solutions that don't really fit the problem. Have you ever seen a program that just needed to raise awareness and communicate some fairly simple information, but featured a needlessly complex learning model filled with interactive case-based branching scenarios? Or one where the desired outcome was a true behavioral change and all the program did was share information? Take care not to over- or under-design for the need you're facing.

As you start making design decisions have these high-level learning patterns in mind. Ask "Is this program mainly about sharing information, building knowledge and skills, solving complex problems, or creating a change in attitude or behavior?"

Let's take a closer look at each of these categories.

Sharing Information

When your goal is to share information or raise awareness, head for *information and communication models*. Here, your design aim is to make it easy for people to get to the main point as quickly as possible and let them explore the topic in whatever depth they want. You want to focus on communication, making use of knowledge mapping, effective web design, and excellent presentation skills.

In *Michael Allen's Guide to E-Learning*, Allen writes that most of what gets created in the name of e-learning and instructional design really falls under the information category: "Sometimes merely the presentation of needed information is sufficient. . . . Persons who are capable of the desired performance and need only some guiding information neither need nor would benefit from instruction. They need only the information" (2003, 277).

When your main goal is to create awareness and knowledge, you're usually not teaching specific skills or processes. So, what's the difference? According to Julie Dirksen, the way to differentiate between a skill and information is simple: just ask yourself, "Is it reasonable to think someone can be proficient without practice?" (2012, 8). If the answer is yes, then you're probably safe with information and awareness models.

An early clue that you might be creating more of an information and awareness piece is if your SME starts throwing around learning objectives like "understand" and "know":

- They need to know that we have a new policy.

- They need to be aware of the risks of clicking on links in emails.

- We want people to know what our divisio
- We need an overview of our products, no skills taught or assessed.
- It's an introduction to our new 401K program.

"Understand" and "know" are lame learning objectives because they're hard to assess. As a responsible instructional designer, you should dig deeper to find out if there's more below the surface. Is there really a skill-based objective that would require some practice? Or is it more complex?

Presentational and informational models are the right choice when the content is simple to understand and the risk due to errors is relatively low. Be prepared to put your marketing hat on—think like an ad agency and write compelling and well-presented content.

Information models work well in e-learning because the learners get to decide what they need to know. Go for user-driven models where the learners can explore the content at their own pace. Think open, browsable experiences like e-magazines and open menus that allow learners to dive into a process or flow. Use models that let people search and explore, browse at their own pace, or just provide a really quick hit of powerful content.

Information and awareness models are appropriate:

- when the content is simple and easy to understand
- when the risk of making mistakes is low

- when information can be easily accessed through performance support tools like job aids at the moment of need
- where true practice isn't required.

You might be saying to yourself, "Well, yeah. Of course we need to raise awareness. But there's more to it! I can't change behavior until I raise awareness." This is true. Sometimes these models get mixed and matched in the big picture that is your overall program—a little bit of this, a little bit of that. None of this is one size fits all, so read on.

Building Skills and Knowledge

Information and communication programs may not have assessable learning objectives, but skill builders definitely do. You need to make sure that the learner comprehends the material and you also need to provide them with the mechanisms to retain this knowledge or skill. If you aim to improve the knowledge and skills of your target audience, then you'll want them to check their understanding and give them feedback on their performance.

You might call this practice. The key here is the application and skill building that the learner can take to the real-world and perform when it matters.

Some examples of skill builders include programs that teach you how to:

- use SalesForce for data mining

- "operate" a medical device, like a ventilator

- speak to the FAA tower on a radio.

Gordon, an instructional designer at a financial services company I work with, quotes Articulate's Tom Kuhlmann in his email signature, with a line that always sticks with me: "People aren't successful because they have information. They're successful because they know how to use it!"

Helping organizations perform better—if that's what you're really trying to do—means giving employees the tools and skills they need to apply all the information you're handing to them. They have to make the connection between the information and what they need to do with it. This may mean providing practice exercises that consolidate understanding and reinforce through repetition and application. If the employee can create strong memories they'll be able to pull up the right information at the right moment of need.

Knowledge and skills builder models are appropriate to use when:

- teaching new processes or procedures

- teaching soft skills like communication or leadership

- practice is necessary in order to reinforce the skills.

Solving Problems and Changing Behaviors

The third reason for creating learning programs is to help people learn how to solve complex problems and change attitudes or behaviors.

This is where things get more complex, and where you tend to see less happening in the e-learning space. In this realm, you're dealing with more complex learning models (which sound like bigger budgets to most people, don't they?), along with situations that may typically benefit from face-to-face feedback, ongoing mentoring, and sustained exposure to new triggers to help create new habits and patterns.

Teaching complex problem solving skills may be a bit more challenging than just teaching someone the six steps to signing into your software system. Complex problem-solving skills require more complex learning models—ones that help the learner explore different consequences, see different outcomes, and experiment a bit.

What about attitude change? If I have a bad attitude about coming into work every day, is that a training problem? Probably not. But, if I have a point of view on diversity in the workplace, then maybe a program designed to change that attitude through awareness-raising exercises and scenarios designed to create empathy would help me change that viewpoint.

I'm particularly interested these days in the line between learning a new skill and changing a behavior. True behavior change can be a long, complex process. Behaviors and habits are set in motion by triggers; for example, you get ready to sit down on the couch and watch a show and you automatically grab a bag of chips on your way to the sofa.

A behavior is how we conduct ourselves. So changing behavior is *changing* how you conduct yourself. It is also often about forming new habits, like remembering to shut the toilet seat, making your bed every morning, or learning to cultivate an attitude of gratitude—every day for the rest of your life.

Behavior change is often conflated or confused with learning a new skill. You can change your habitual behavior by referring to a job aid or a cheat sheet. For instance, I can teach someone the four steps to being a better listener or sharing feedback with an employee in a difficult situation. Over time, as this new skill becomes automatic, fully ingrained, and habitual, we could say we have created a new behavior. Conversely, changing an existing behavior may require unlearning a pre-existing skill or changing an attitude or mindset. This is the hard stuff.

Most e-learning doesn't really focus on behavior or attitude change. To change behavior, you might think about B.F. Skinner's behaviorism model or cognitive behavioral therapy. These are systems of behavioral change that happen over long durations. The context of a 30-minute e-learning program lacks the personal element and sustained commitment that is typically required for a behavior change. Real behavior change requires new habit formation, reflective consideration of ones motives, and reasons for change. It takes real commitment, intrinsic desire, and sustained effort over time with periodic refreshers. Or, a really good carrot or stick.

When trying to change behaviors, it certainly helps if you create good awareness and desire to change. Sometimes that's enough. Think about the Public Service Announcement–style ad campaign or a really powerful documentary on the dangers of texting and driving. Sometimes, behavior change is inspired the most by a strong emotional message that motivates people to change their own behaviors.

To assist some behavior changes, you'll also need to provide opportunities to practice. E-learning is a great opportunity for this, because branching exercises and immersive simulations allow the user to experience the consequences of making a particular mistake. When you experience first-hand the results of your own knowledge gaps or an inappropriate mindset, you are more likely to see the logic of changing your ways.

Use complex problem solving and behavior change models to:

- teach the thought process that a 10-year veteran uses to trouble-shoot a product to new technicians

- help identify, tackle, and eradicate unhealthy attitudes and foster harmony in a multicultural society

- improve workplace cultures and behaviors by increasing knowledge, understanding, and training skills within this area.

In a Facebook conversation I had with Koreen Olbrish, senior project manager at Lynda.com and author of *Immersive Learning*, we talked about e-learning, behavior change, and the reality of what typically happens in organizations. She wrote:

Sales training's goal is to improve sales numbers and they think the way to do that is by training the reps to be better salespeople. Do I think their design supports behavior change? No. Do I think that's their goal? Yes. If they really wanted to change behavior, they would design for practice and role play/simulation in context. Mostly what they do is e-learning, with some verbalizations and role play with peers. So, the question is: Do you want to know what the goal of the training is, or do want to know what training is designed to actually do? There is a difference in intent versus execution.

So the question is, how do you intend to support behavior change in your organization in a meaningful way? How will you align your intent with your execution?

One Learning Designer's View

In October 2013, I ran an anonymous poll on my blog about e-learning and when we use it. One of the questions I asked was about using e-learning to change attitudes. The following response was my favorite:

> We still struggle with attitude change regarding good learning events in my organization. I want to create learning events that focus on skill building, attitude, performance change, and so forth, to engage and motivate our learners, but it can be an uphill battle. I find that it's generally not the learners or even their managers who are most skeptical, but more likely it's the people who have been performing "training" for years. Some completely refuse to entertain new ideas and pull up their 100-slide deck of bulleted PowerPoints. More frustrating though, are those who say, "Yes, yes, we are learning professionals this is what we want to do!" — and then go back to their wordy PowerPoints and "annual reviews." Am I venting? I think there is still a real disconnect in the learning industry (not just in my organization) between what people talk about, say they believe, and what they really deliver to learners.

Some Models You Can Try Out

So, what do these models look like?

The rest of this chapter outlines several different instructional design models. They're roughly organized from awareness to skill builder to behavior change, but these categories aren't strict. You'll find overlap and ways to mix and match based on what you're trying to achieve and to suit the specific learning requirements and the context or nature of the target audience. After all, you will often need to impart knowledge for learners to apply during a role play or simulation, so you may find yourself building a knowledge and skill-builder model followed by a goal-based scenario.

Consider these examples a starting point, and not an exhaustive list of all the things you can do. These are things I find myself pulling out of my toolkit frequently—particularly on projects that need to be created on a tight timeline. You may have your own that you could add to this pile. And hopefully I'll have more of my own as the years go by, too.

The Infomercial

When you need to get a point across and quickly, you could be best served by creating a short video. Think YouTube or infomercial—two to five minutes of really good content presentation that provides an overview of the new business process or explains what a department does. It could be a snazzy TV commercial approach to create awareness about a new brand or an initiative within your organization. Three minutes could be much more effective than a 30-minute e-learning program!

Your infomercial could easily be the first section of a bigger program or it could be something you share with people as needed.

I recently created an infomercial-style overview of a company's new learning management system that would be targeted toward its suppliers. The company wanted to use the video as a way to create awareness of the initiative and get people to start thinking internally about how they could leverage it to drive more sales, improve processes, and provide better education to their customers. Key people moved through the organization with this video loaded on their iPads. They could pause and have discussions, using the video to spark conversation.

You can use it:

- when you want to make a big impact in a short amount of time

- when you want to create an asset that you can reuse in bigger programs

- when you want to spark conversation and share ideas.

Search and Find

In the Google world in which we live, a lot of people prefer to search and find the resources and information they need to solve their problems. As instructional designers, your job may be to collect and target the better information out there and pull it together into a resource portal that people can search and explore as they wish. So go out and find articles, resources, PDF, and links to serve up to people on a particular subject.

You can use it:

- for a more expert audience who knows the basics and wants to dig deeper into the subject

- for an audience who wants more control over their experience; this allows people to make adult decisions about where to spend their time.

Explore the Process

Let's say you want to create awareness and share information about a new workflow or process. Maybe it's a change to an existing workflow and it makes sense to give people the ability to jump around and get just what they need, rather than trying to force feed them every single step of the process. Within a structured e-learning program (a.k.a., a "course") you can provide an open framework or menu structure that people can dip in and out of at will. They can drill down into that process and learn more about each step, but you don't lock them into a set flow. Most adults like to explore and don't want to be treated like children. An open and exploratory model gives people choices.

You can use it:

- for refresher training on a new process or workflow so people can drill down where they need to

- for more expert or advanced learners who already know enough on a topic to know what questions they might have.

Job Aids and Performance Support

Job aids and performance support are great examples of information-based learning materials. Give the people what they want, when they want it. In these situations, they don't want banks of questions to test their understanding at the end. They want a brief announcement of what they need to know and the ability to dip in and out to get some short tips or recall some key principles or steps. This could look like a job aid with easy-to-follow steps, or a visual depiction of a process. (Short YouTube video tutorials and SnapGuides are great examples!)

You can use it:

- when people need to quickly get their hands on information and tips

- as refresher training

- if it's a skill that people won't use very often and thus won't have practiced to the point of habit

- when the risk of doing it wrong is high and you want to make sure people have a guide they can follow to do it properly.

The E-Magazine or the E-Book

I love reading books (in hard copy or on my tablet). I also enjoy reading magazines and newspapers. And you know what? I actually learn from them. And so can your people!

An e-magazine or e-book style is a great way to present information in a structured, indexed format. Let people flip through the electronic pages at will. Include beautiful graphics and diagrams to illustrate a process flow, capture video or audio testimonials of experts sharing their insights, and write short and snappy copy to make your point.

An attendee at a presentation I gave on learning models shared that she had created an e-book for senior leaders, which was used as a browsable prework component before a two-day on-site collaborative workshop. The e-book included video tours of their campus, articles and opinions, and lots of assets for people to explore and digest in their own way. She said it was really well-received, and no wonder—it allowed people to make decisions about what was most relevant to them. Personalization in learning may be the new buzzword; letting people choose their own path through the content lets them do just that.

You can use it:

- to create awareness about a new policy or program that's rolling out

- as part of an onboarding program for new hires

- as part of a broader learning campaign that includes other training assets down the line, such as a tutorials or more detailed how-tos.

Knowledge and Skill Builder

The base entry point and time-honored approach is the classic tutorial structure, which at Kineo we call a knowledge and skill builder. It will get a longer description here than the other learning models because there's a bit more to cover and it's really good foundational stuff for learning designers.

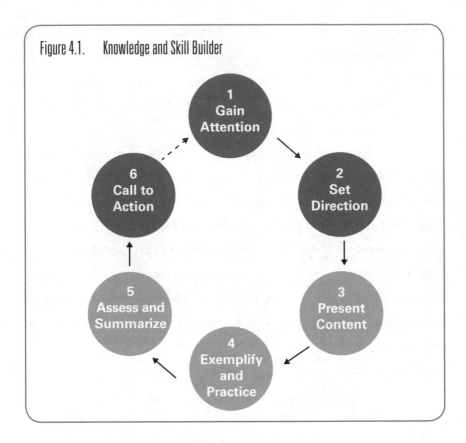

Figure 4.1.   Knowledge and Skill Builder

The knowledge and skill builder is generally seen as having the most straightforward and simple format. With this model, we follow a standard sequence to systematically build knowledge and get learners to demonstrate understanding.

If you have been around the instructional design block a few times, you might see some similarities with Gagné's Nine Events of Instruction, which are:

1. Gain attention.

2. Describe the goal.

3. Stimulate recall of prior knowledge.

4. Present the material to be learned.

5. Provide guidance for learning.

6. Elicit performance "practice."

7. Provide informative feedback.

8. Assess performance test.

9. Enhance retention and transfer.

The knowledge and skill builder condenses the nine events and gives us a simple and effective blueprint that works for probably 70 percent of the e-learning programs created to help people learn a new skill.

1. Gain attention: Hook the learners with something good, something that will make them sit up in their seat, lean in, and pay attention. Chapter 5 will talk all about hooking people in so stay tuned for more ideas.

2. Set direction: Let the learners know where they're going on this journey and what they're going to get out of it. Here you convey that "what's in it for me?" bit. Also be sure to let them know how long it will take, so they can plan accordingly. *(Objectives)*

3. Present: This is where your content lives, laid out in a thoughtful and interesting way, rather than just a dump of 43 slides of text bullets. Use questions and interactions to present information (questions aren't just for tests), allowing the person to learn through discovery. Use stories to add context and present the information in a way that allows the individual to construct some personal meaning and identify how he or she can apply the content. What you choose to present, and how, is what makes one learning experience fundamentally different from the next.

4. Exemplify and practice: Now you're ready to help consolidate their learning with case studies or stories that exemplify this content in the real world, and practice exercise that can help reinforce their skills. This is where many learners truly begin to get it, especially those who struggle with pure concepts.

Be sure to provide opportunities to practice using relevant activities and exercises. See chapter 6 for some ideas.

5. Assess and summarize: Test and provide a thoughtful summary of the key takeaways from the program.

Final tests and quizzes can be useful for people to confirm that they have achieved the learning objectives. This, in its own right, builds confidence. From an organizational point of view, testing is a good way of checking if the overall program has delivered the agreed learning goals. However, don't let these test or quizzes serve as the final word on whether or not someone has actually learned anything from your experience. The true test, ultimately, will be in performance on the job.

Be sure to provide one final chance for people to get the key messages again; this is traditionally referred to as the "tell them what you told them" part of the process. Summarize the key learning points, but also leave space for the learner to reflect. A good way to do this is to encourage them to think of what they will do differently, which leads us to the last step of a formal training program.

6. Call to action: Finish the experience by making sure people go away with a clear call to action. They should know what they need to do to apply what they have learned. Putting forth a call to action helps the person remember that the learning process doesn't end with the final click in the course. The call to action provides a launch pad to start applying those skills and ideas in the workplace.

Your call to action should challenge people to reflect on their current way of doing things and make a commitment to change when necessary. A simple, "What are you going to start, stop, and continue?" question can get the wheels of change rolling. Other options could involve action plans, affirmations, or new SMART goals.

One of your calls to action may be a nod to the additional information out there that you would love for them to explore; perhaps what your stakeholders wanted you to cover, but that you persuaded them not to. You can provide links and give recommendations for deeper exploration and let people know where to go if they need more help.

The call to action sets the stage for the person's next steps, helping her develop a game plan to follow on the job. It could involve a refresher module or a webinar. An interactive coach is another good option, because the coach will help her reflect on and tweak her action plan by asking the right questions and responding to her answers.

You may also consider adding a human component to this call to action—perhaps having your LMS trigger a review session with her manager two weeks after she completes the program.

The call to action gives the learner some direction for what to do next, helping her think about what actions and tasks to focus on. Remember, it's what happens next—in the real world—that really counts.

The knowledge and skill builder model can be used for an entire course, but also for the discrete chunks within the course. If you've broken up a 30-minute program into three sections, you can follow this model for each section. It's a versatile approach that works well for all audiences, especially for novices to a subject or as part of a basic foundation learning program.

You can use it:

- for a lot of your e-learning programs

- when teaching technical policies, processes and procedures, and some soft skills that require practice

- if you need a solid model for a rapid design process

- as a checklist to make sure your program covers some basic steps that will ensure better knowledge transfer and retention.

Show Me, Try it, Test Me

The mainstay of process and systems training for many years (both online and face-to-face) is usually referred to as show me, try it, test me.

In this model, you give the learner the chance to learn through observation (show me), then practice it on their own with guided prompts and feedback from the program (try it). The final section (test me) lets the learner run through the process on his own with little input from the system—in more of a simulation or sandbox environment.

Off-the-shelf tools like Adobe Captivate and Articulate Storyline incorporate this model right into their software, making it easy to build and execute.

You can use it:

- for software tutorials
- for non-software processes like filling out a form or completing steps in a process.

Just the Facts, Ma'am

Sometimes you really just want to get the information out there as succinctly as possible. Maybe the lawyers say this content absolutely has to be in the course. I call this approach "just the facts, ma'am."

Just the facts is a design structure you can use to share facts, knowledge, and information in a compact and reusable format. You might even call it a consolidated information dump, and you wouldn't be wrong because you're squeezing key information into a few screens in what is probably a linear format. It's really an information and communication model. Within a longer course you could include a short just the facts topic as a precursor to a more complex goal-based scenario or a guided story.

This model would work well for product knowledge, using short standalone modules to share information about a series of products. For each product, you could answer some key questions like:

- What is it?

- How does it work?

- Who is it good for?

- How do I sell it?

The learners need to be able to accurately describe the features and benefits of their products and this baseline knowledge enables them to properly sell the right product to the right customer.

You can use it to:

- communicate facts and information

- share new information, such as product knowledge, a new policy, or an overview of a process

- create a series of short, quick hit e-learning objects that could be linked to from an LMS or webpage and be very easy to reuse and repurpose.

Guided Stories

More and more learning designers (including myself) are hooked on stories. Conventional wisdom says that we learn better from stories, so it's one thing to embed stories and examples in your course, but it's another to build the entire course around the story. That's what the guided story model is all about.

 Meet Pete. He's a learning designer at a small manufacturing organization and he's trying to find ways to deliver better e-learning to his colleagues so they can cut down on costly mistakes and gain more efficiency. In this short program, we'll follow Pete on his journey from accidental instructional designer to superstar (and learn a few tricks along the way).

benefit of story

In a guided story, you reveal course content through the lens of an individual in a "day in the life" or a "year in the life" format. This provides an opportunity to learn through observation, experience someone else's mistakes, see the consequences, and then relate the experience back to your own world.

I'm currently designing a program on information security for a large organization. We've got 15 minutes to create some awareness and drive home a few key points. Rather than dump screen after screen of information, we're going to tell the story of Joe and his horrible, no good, very bad day. It starts off when he leaves his personal iPad on the table of a coffee shop to reserve a spot while he waits in line. He comes back only to find, surprise, that his iPad is gone! What unfolds are a series of blunders (and their consequences) that Joe makes throughout the day, from clicking on bad links to posting vacation photos on Twitter while his house gets robbed. It's a much more memorable way to make a few key points than just using bulleted lists and boring text screens full of policies and facts. By putting the information into the context of a story, you help people see exactly how this information applies to them and their world.

You can use it:

- almost any time
- in both infomercials to add context to a short video, or as your overall narrative force in a knowledge and skill builder.

See It in Action

This model works well to demonstrate someone doing a process or perhaps having a specific kind of conversation—such as a job interview or a feedback session with an employee. You can demonstrate the scene done poorly— highlighting mistakes that people typically make and so they can learn to avoid the consequences—or model optimal performance. You could create a short animated sequence, shoot live action video, or create text and graphic screens that show what happened.

You can use it:

- for demonstrating soft skills

- to prepare people for classroom sessions where they will be expected to role play situations in front of an audience to get specific feedback on their own performance

- to model optimal performance.

The Think Aloud

Rather than just see someone do the steps, why not have them explain what they're doing and the thinking process behind the choices they make? A think aloud is more than a demonstration, as you hear the whys behind the actions. Jane Bozarth writes about "showing your work" as a way to build knowledge in an organization, share expertise, and help other people avoid the mistakes you might have made. Think alouds are a great way to show your work.

You can use it:

- as a performance support tool (think YouTube video of someone showing you how they fixed that leaky faucet)

- when you want to illustrate the thinking that goes into solving a problem (like explaining how to fix a complex software system.)

Sharing Expert Views

Much of an organization's knowledge is held in the heads of a few experts. Instead of trying to paraphrase what you think they might say, go out and capture them saying it!

how indexers think,.

Create a podcast or video library of interviews with experts. This could be a page in your e-learning program with pictures of four people that each play a 30-second video clip of them sharing their top tips for sales. Have people capture and record how they complete a specific task using a screencasting tool like SnagIt or Camtasia. As they demonstrate the task, have them provide audio commentary in a "think aloud" format: "Here's what I'm doing now and this is why I'm doing it this way and these are some of the things I ask myself as I'm doing it."

Social and collaborative business tools make creating and sharing user-generated content really easy. You may want to liberate this type of expert content from your authoring tool and instead host it through a collaborative platform like SharePoint or Jive to make it easy to share throughout your organization. The point is to get these viewpoints out of people's heads and into a discoverable and shareable format.

Don't forget about capturing the viewpoints of your customers. Building that empathic connection through hearing what customers really like or don't like from your company serves as a powerful reminder and message to keep your people performing at their best.

You can use it:

- when you want to show a particular point of view to your audience
- to show thought processes behind complex problem solving skills, allowing people to extrapolate from the expert's situations to their own.

Learn and Apply

Learn and apply gives someone a choice in the route they take through the content. At the opening screen, let the learner choose: learn or apply?

Think you know it already? Then jump right in and try it out a simulation! See if you can apply what you know through scenario-based exercises and questions. Should you struggle in an area, you will be routed to the appropriate learning content. (Once learners can clearly see their own knowledge gap, you may have their undivided attention.)

Not so confident or prefer to start with the information and then try it out? Start with the learn section instead. Here you'll find traditional e-learning show and tell screens. Once you have viewed all the learning content, you will be routed to the apply section to try it out.

This model has a lot in common with goal-based scenarios, although it's a little different in that the learner can choose the information path as a learning track (whereas in a goal-based scenario the information is accessed more as reference materials).

It is also similar to a full branching simulation approach, but the model is designed so that if the learner makes a mistake in the scenario he will be brought to a discrete, relevant section of the tutorials. Once he completes the relevant module, he can then return to the question he got wrong and see if he can continue without making further mistakes.

You can use it:

- when you want to give people a choice in how they go through the program

- when you think people will think they know it all and be eager to prove themselves without having to go through all the content.

Fake Branching

Unlike a more complex branching exercise that allows you to go down different paths, the fake branching exercise sets up decision points, but moves the story along in the same direction regardless of the learner's response. Feedback for each response shows the consequence of that decision and explains why a certain choice was not the right one to make. You might ask the learner to keep trying until she gets it right, or you might tell her the best choice and move the story along as if that choice had been made.

This model lets the learner see the story play out to its best conclusion, but gets her thinking about what to do at those key decision points. For example, let's say you want to teach a competency-based interviewing process. So you explain some of the basic skills and information, and then you drop them into a scenario. Using still photos and audio with simple image transitions to simulate the feeling of a live conversation, you see (and hear) Sarah interviewing Thomas for a key position within her group.

But instead of making this a passive watch and listen experience, the conversation stops, and the learner has to apply what she knows about the interviewing process and decide what to do next. "What should Sarah say now to best move the conversation forward?" The learner then chooses the best response from a series of plausible options.

Customized feedback for each response helps you address common mistakes and misperceptions. "While that might be a good option because of [*a sound reason*] that approach could make her defensive. We think the third choice is the best response because it does [*explanation*]. Continue to see what happens."

The scenario continues in the same linear path following the learner's response, but there is some feeling of consequence or impact of having chosen the wrong answer.

This approach is all about the quality of the feedback you give and the plausibility of the choices. You need to have both here—it only works if the learner has to really stop and consider the actions, because there's no obvious right or wrong way to go. You'll spend the most time on this part of the design: working closely with your subject matter expert to make sure the choices are all realistic. The best questions challenge us and make us think. Make the learner work for that payoff!

You can use it:

- to model an overall process from start to finish in the best possible way

- when you want people to consider key decision points in a process

- if you don't have time to create a full-branching program.

Goal-Based Scenarios (Full Branching)

A scenario-based learning (or learn-by-doing or goal-based task) approach is a great way to explore a topic more fully for a knowledge or skills-based learning experience. It is also especially useful for changing attitudes and behavior. If learners see the consequences of gaps in knowledge or an inappropriate mindset, they are more likely to see the logic of making a change.

In a goal-based scenario, you drop the learner into a situation and assign him a role. "You are a salesperson at a local branch of Excalibur Bank. It's a busy day in the branch. You're sitting down with a customer who wants to open a savings account. So what should you say first?"

As the learner makes decisions, the story changes. A full branching exercise is e-learning in the form of a "choose your own adventure story," which I enjoy reading with my kids today: "If you go to the Mayan temple with Phillipe, turn to page 12. If you stay in the car with Juanita, turn to page 18." It's an exciting way to read; every choice leads to a different twist and a different outcome.

Branching exercises let people choose from a few options and then experience the consequences of their decisions. It's a good approach to take when there are a lot of gray areas around a topic and not necessarily a clear right or wrong answer. This could be a good way to let people experience a job interview process firsthand and see how different kinds of questions can lead to a different understanding of the job applicant.

You can use a branching exercise to practice a skill, but you can go beyond that, into behavior change by having some hidden objectives. For instance, maybe your bank scenario seems to be about getting the customer served as quickly as possible, because the branch was very busy. But you were really trying to make sure the person took the time to adequately fact find, even when rushed!

From a development perspective, this type of program makes some people nervous. "It'll take too much programming! It's too expensive! It'll take too much time!" And while that may be true, it may also be the right design path—especially when you think experiencing the consequences are a crucial part of the learning process.

Off-the-shelf authoring tools like Articulate Storyline enable easy development of branching stories. The programming element no longer an excuse, you may still hesitate over the time involved to design and write all the different branches of that story. I can't provide an easy solution to that, but good design does take time.

A branching scenario provides a great place for the learner to make mistakes along the way, see what happens, and then try it again another way. Half the fun of working through a branching scenario is going down the road you know you shouldn't take, just to see what happens. It's like sanctioned naughtiness.

As you design a branching program, first set out the "perfect route." That is, go through the entire scenario the "right" way (if there is one right way). Get that down on paper, and then do some critical error analysis to find those natural points where learners diverge from the yellow brick road.

You can use it:

- to let people experience different outcomes or try different approaches

- when it's important that people experience the consequences of wrong choices (rather than just being told)

- for the contextual practice of a skill

- to explore how different attitudes can change the outcome of a situation.

Investigate and Decide

Investigate and decide is a type of goal-based scenario used to provide practice in evidenced-based decision making.

The learner is given a mission or goal and access to supporting resources that contain evidence to inform a decision or series of decisions. That is, the learner must investigate the resources to decide on a course of action.

To move through the experience, the learner makes a series of decisions—just like in the real world. Along the way, he is given access to supporting materials that he may need to use to determine the best course of action or to justify his decision. Supporting material could include simulated work documents (emails, reports), video clips, expert testimony, links to policies, FAQs, and so on. An investigate and decide scenario is really about solving a problem and using resources to make an informed decision.

The situation may not have one absolute right outcome, but rather a series of judgments that the learner has to make throughout a process.

You can use it:

- to teach complex problem solving skills

- to create a learning experience in which the learner has to dive right into a situation

- for a more experienced audience who already feels it "knows" the subject.

Is That All There Is?

Of course not. This list is not exhaustive. But these models should be enough to get you started and I trust you have your own models that you would add to this list. Go out and look for any inspiration and ideas that you can add to your toolkit. Here are a few places you can go:

Most e-learning custom content suppliers provide demos and showcase sites where you can access their ideas.

E-learning authoring tool companies have blogs and communities showcasing their examples. The Articulate e-Learning Heroes community is particularly active, with loads of people just like you sharing ideas and examples.

E-learning and training conferences often have a demofest as part of the conference. The eLearning Guild has run a really popular demofest every year at its DevLearn and Learning Solutions conferences and usually does follow-up webinars showcasing the winners.

chapter 5

Finding Your Hook

In this chapter . . .

- Why is grabbing the learner's attention early so vital?

- What strategies and tips can you use to hook your audience?

- How do you keep people motivated to stick around?

The beginning. This is where your e-learning program needs to reach out and pull someone into the program in a meaningful way.

When you attract and sustain someone's attention, you get very different results than when you force them to sit in front of your screen with their eyes peeled open clockwork orange style. When you attract someone's attention they're going to want to stick around to see what you have to say; their curiosity is piqued, their radars are up, and they want to know what's going to happen next.

Essentially, finding your hook means tapping in to what motivates people. We've got to think like marketing and sales people—we are essentially selling content—and convince the learner that's it really is going to be worth her precious time and attention. There's a lot going on in this world. Why should she stick around in the first place? And then what's going to keep her there until the very end?

Let's dip into a little bit of learning theory for a moment. John Keller, a professor of instructional systems and educational psychology at Florida State University, developed the ARCS Model of Motivational Design, which defines four categories of motivational variables: attention, relevance, confidence, and satisfaction. According to Keller, these variables connect instruction to the goals of learners by appropriately stimulating and challenging them and influencing how they feel after achieving (or failing to meet) their learning goal.

ARCS helps instructional designers think about how to answer a few key questions:

- How do we make instruction more appealing?

- What makes a learner eager and willing to sit through an e-learning program?

- How do you keep the learner interested?

- How do you make sure he knows what's going on and what to expect?

- How does the learner know that his time was well spent?

While we can load up courses with bells and whistles to make them tons o' fun, that's not the best way to get attention in a meaningful way. All those seductive details may end up doing more damage through distraction and learner fatigue than we intend. Instead, we should find strategies and tactics that support instructional goals. Remember, it's training, not entertainment. ARCS can keep us focused on what matters for the instructional experience and is a great model to help you focus your scripting efforts. I'm not going to go into great depth about the complete ARCS model here, but I do want to focus on that critical A for *attention*.

Keller breaks attention down into three subcategories: perceptual arousal, inquiry arousal, and variability. Think how you can build these techniques as you craft an e-learning script that makes people sit up, lean in, and listen. Let's break the attention category down now, one at a time.

Open Their Eyes

Perceptual arousal is about creating awareness and getting people to notice you in the first place. To create perceptual arousal, you might turn a topic on its head in a surprising way or present a startling fact or statistic. Go for the unexpected. Introduce the novel, the surprising, the shocking.

The most tried-and-true method of this in compliance courses is the standard headline screen that opens the course. You know what I'm talking about? Torn scraps of newspaper that show the hefty fines that other financial organizations had to pay when a particular policy was not followed. It might be a cliché in compliance courses, but it does work to raise eyebrows and demonstrate the real stakes at play.

When we tell stories of what can go wrong, we tap into a primal human need to pay attention to gossip. Try opening your next program with the story of someone who really blew it. How about the story of Tim?

Tim was a hair stylist who was always trying out the newest products. Unfortunately, one day he failed to learn how a new and exciting hair care product really worked before applying it to his customer Janet's hair. The result? Orange hair, a really unhappy customer, lost sales, and a tarnished reputation. Want to make sure that doesn't happen to you? Then stick around and we'll show you how to master the product.

The story of Tim and what went wrong raises the learner's awareness of what can happen if she doesn't master this content. She can imagine herself in Tim's place and feel how awful that would be. Through his mistake, she gets an eye to what she wants to avoid. She might feel embarrassed or horrified for Tim, and feel really bad for Janet, whose hair looks truly awful. She's made an emotional connection to this content—she feels a little uncomfortable and wants to pay attention to what's coming next so she can be sure she doesn't do this to any of her customers.

In 2007, I attended my first eLearning Guild conference and heard Clark Quinn speak. It was the first time I'd heard someone use the term "wiffem." Say what? Oh, WIIFM—what's in it for me. This was an accidental instructional designer moment, where bells went off in my head and a few things clicked.

Making it emotional doesn't mean creating a tear jerker e-learning program à la *Gone With the Wind*. It means getting people to care—which is the heart of identifying the what's in it for me. When we put forth the WIIFM, we help people make a truly emotional connection: Why do I even care about any of this? Why does it matter to me?

We need people to care about this content, not because we simply want them to like our e-learning design, but because we want them to take action. You want them to pay attention, learn a skill, and change their behavior. By focusing on the WIIFM, you help people see why this matters to their lives, and what the risk is if they don't do this right.

Chip and Dan Heath, in *Made to Stick: Why Some Ideas Survive and Others Die*, remind us that the "goal of making messages 'emotional' is to make people care. Feelings inspire people to act" (2008, 169).

When you write your next e-learning script think about these questions: What stories can you tell on your opening screen to get people to notice? What surprising facts or stats can you spring on them? What can you do to create an unexpected scene in your e-learning program?

Just don't forget to keep it relevant to the content. Remember, relevance is the "R" in ARCS and ensures that you're helping the learners connect the content to their own experience and create retrieval hooks so they can apply the information in the appropriate context.

Be sure to take time to study the ARCS model in more depth on your own time. I've given you a taste of the "A" and the "R," but hopefully I've left you wanting more.

In the meantime, what else can you do in your e-learning programs to get people to sit up and pay attention?

Incite Curiosity

Inquiring minds want to know, so inject a little inquiry arousal. Ask some hard questions and put forth some real-life problems that the learner might want to solve. Get him curious and wanting to know more.

Take the commercial for the 10 p.m. news, for example. It pulls us in with the quick plug, "Find out the three ways that your sink can kill you!" We stick around waiting to find out, because with a headline that titillating, we've got to find out what it is all about.

According to Chip and Dan Heath, when we feel a gap in our knowledge about something, it makes us curious, thus making the content stickier because we want to fill that knowledge gap. It's why we sit through the entire episode of *CSI* to find out who did it or keep reading each 1,000-plus page book in the *Game of Thrones* series. We simply need to know what's going to happen!

In your next e-learning script, think about creating a series of cliffhangers to insight curiosity in your learners. Introduce a character or a work place dilemma or situation on the first screen of the course. Then, make something intriguing happen, but leave the learners hanging while you move to the next parts of the course. Come back to the story periodically to find out what happened, weaving facts and content around their story. Have the learner fill the content gaps by discovering the answers.

Make sure you ask questions to expose your learner's knowledge gap. Pose a series of questions at the beginning of the course that people are likely to get wrong. Confront them with the reality of what they're missing and get them motivated to fill that gap. You can't just tell people the facts, they have to realize that they actually need them.

Variability

Keller's third subcategory under attention is variability. This means turning on the beat box and mixing it up. In other words, stop boring people to death with screen after screen of the exact same thing. Find ways to present your content differently—try using a combination of video, animation, and text. Throw in an exercise when they least expect it. Make each page a new surprise and keep them guessing.

Do your best to avoid creating a page of text bullets followed by a page of text bullets followed by yet another page of text bullets. This doesn't mean avoiding templates or reusing screen types. In fact, I'm all for reusing

6 - 7

screen types. At Kineo, we expect to use about six to seven unique screen types over the course of a 20-screen, slide-based e-learning program. Reusing saves time and production costs, as well as adding a level of consistency throughout the program. Variability is good, but too much variability can create a chaotic and unordered experience.

Find ways to mix up your screen types and layouts and don't present screen after screen of the same old format. Surprise people by throwing in a question or exercise after a few content screens to help them engage more deeply in the experience and give them a chance to consolidate their understanding.

AIDA: Attention, Interest, Desire, Action ⭐ →linear

E-learning programs have a lot of competition out there. An employee may need to take a 20-minute program on health and safety, but the lure of other shiny objects is strong—work deadlines, websites, social networking applications, the guy in the next cubical.

Who's got it figured out? The advertisers! TV commercials and prints ads have a way of drawing us in, capturing our interest, creating the desire, and then—when they're really good—getting us to make the big purchase. Let's explore AIDA, a classic copywriting model, and think about how we can apply it to e-learning projects. When Kineo's Mark Harrison turned me onto this model, I thought he was talking about opera. I've since taken a closer look and think that all e-learning designers should be swiping a few pages from the marketing team.

What Is AIDA?

AIDA stands for attention, interest, desire, and action, and can be used to describe the sequence of events that goes into making someone want to buy your product or service.

Now I know what you're thinking: that's completely different from e-learning! E-learning isn't about buying and selling stuff.

But isn't it? We need to think of e-learning as selling itself—it needs to be compelling and the content needs to grab the learner and sustain her interest.

So let's break AIDA down.

Attention

What's your hook? How do you pull the learner in and get him to sit up and notice your program in the first place?

A simple way to grab attention in print media is with a great headline. In e-learning that's the title of your course. Instead of calling the course "Customer Service Basics," call it "Five Ways to Make Your Customers Smile." Put the "what's in it for me" factor out on the table as early as you can.

As we've already discussed, get the learner's attention early and often. Tell shocking stories, share powerful statistics, and ask questions to get them engaged. Use emotion to connect with the learners, get them to pay attention, and then get them to stay.

Interest

In AIDA, you capture a potential customer's interest by focusing on the advantages and benefits of your product and service, not by doing a feature dump.

In e-learning you can do the same—avoid the feature dump (leave that to a job aid), and instead keep the focus on the "why this matters" part. How are you going to use this new process to speed up your sales cycle and get better results?

Desire

Great advertisers play to our desires. "If you use our product you'll be sexier, stronger, smarter, and really, really cool." Smart consumers know what's going on, but even the clever ones are susceptible to the message.

In e-learning you're not creating a desire to buy, but rather a desire to change behavior, follow the new process, move forward, and learn. Incite desire and inspire: "You'll make fewer errors, be more efficient, and get to go home earlier!"

Action

In copywriting, the final "A" stands for action. This is the bit about getting the consumer to go out and buy that new car. "Call now and for just $19.99, you'll also get a free knife!"

At the end of an e-learning program, you want them to go out and do something. Send your people off with a final call to action: practice the new process on the live system with your manager; make three cold calls today; set up an account on a social networking site and send a practice message.

It's a Sequence

The mistake most e-learning makes? We attract attention with some intriguing statistic, but then skip the interest and desire steps. This does little more than create a sense of intrigue, but creates little to no interest or desire to stick around and commit to completing the e-learning. We then dive straight to the presentation and action stage.

How can you avoid that? Don't think of AIDA as a checklist—it's not "as long as I cover those four I will be OK", but rather a well-structured linear sequence that taps into the hearts and minds of your audience. Cover the entire A-I-D bit up front. If you don't get to the D stage right at the start, they won't bother going through the rest of the module.

Of course, don't forget the instructional part! This is e-learning after all. The meat of your program—the knowledge—should reinforce the desire by constantly showing the benefits of changing your ways. This then leads to the final section, the Action stage.

Start Using AIDA Today!

So there's there info. Your call to action?

1. Start watching *Mad Men* and learn a thing or two from Don Draper.

2. Analyze a TV commercial or print AD—how are they using AIDA?

3. As you write your next e-learning program, apply AIDA to your design and writing.

Object to Learning Objectives

Do your e-learning programs typically start with something like this?

After reading this section, you will be able to:

- Explain two of the reasons why I don't like traditional learning objectives.

- Describe your own view of learning objectives.

- Develop an alternative approach to listing learning objectives in your next e-learning course.

Quite gripping, isn't it? Let's talk about some other options.

Objection, Your Honor!

Learning objectives do have value, at least from the instructional designer's and the business's point of view. They define what you, the instructional designer, wants to help the learner be able to DO at the end of the program so that you can identify the specific content necessary to support those objectives as well as practice exercises to support the consolidation of that learning. What exactly are you trying to teach?

Will Thalheimer, who created a new taxonomy for learning objective, labels this type of objective an instructional-design objective, which is "a statement developed by and for instructional designers to guide the design and development of learning and instruction" (2006).

So, we do need them, but most people find them painful to read. One could argue that most learners don't even bother reading them.

Michael Allen states that lists of learning objectives aren't motivating. However, he also says that "measurable behavioral objectives are, indeed, critical components to guide the design of effective training applications" (2003, 160). Unfortunately, there's nothing that will get people to yawn more quickly than a list of them. More often than not, learning objectives sound like they were written by robots. How about you? Do you take the time to read those objectives? Really?

Break the Rules

One approach, as Cathy Moore demonstrates so well, is to write better objectives. In her post, "Makeover: Turn Objectives into Motivators," she transforms boring objectives like "describe how vocal tone affects customer rapport," into "use your tone of voice to build rapport with customers." By personalizing the language, changing "I-know-it verbs" into "I-can-change-the-world verbs," and making the objective more concrete, she presents an objective that the learner can actually understand and do something with.

Thalheimer would call this a focusing objective, "a statement presented to learners before they encounter learning material—provided to help guide learner attention the most important aspects of that learning material" (2006).

Michael Allen thinks better-written objectives are a start, but wonders if any form of the "textual listing of objectives [is] really the best way to sell anyone on learning" (2003, 161). He urges instructional designers to break the rules: "Don't list objectives." Instead, provide some meaningful and memorable experiences using interactivity, graphics, animation, and story-telling. Ask questions that pique the learner's interest and get them focused.

Change things up a bit. Lose the text bullets written with the required verbs from Bloom's Taxonomy. Help the learner organize the learning experience, but do it in a more interesting way.

Allen suggests some alternatives to listing out boring learning objectives in text bullet form:

- **Put the learner to work:** Have the learner attempt a task. If they fail, they'll know what they should be able to do when they finish your program (hopefully, complete that task).

- **Use drama:** Create a scenario showing the risk of what could happen if the learner doesn't learn the content—and the benefits that will happen when they do.

- **Create a game quiz:** Instead of a traditional boring assessment, create a game-like quiz. Based on their performance, learners will see if they are beginners or advanced, and where their gaps in knowledge might lie. And they'll be able to see what kinds of tasks they should be able to do at the end of the course. Just make sure that the game you design has relevance and doesn't add to the distraction or disconnect.

In *Brain Rules*, John Medina tells us that emotionally charged events are more memorable than neutral ones. We're primed to retain the "gist"— the memorable, emotional impression of something—and not all of the details. To keep people engaged and focused, we need to re-hook them

every 10 minutes. The brain needs those breaks, so consider chunking a program into short 10-minute chapters or sections. At the beginning of each new section, come back at 'em with a strong story or an emotional hook to reel them back in.

So, you got some ideas you can put into action? Bottom line, begin with a bang. Avoid the blah-blah-blah and help people see why these programs matter. Go forth into the world and consider the beginnings of TV shows, books, articles, and e-learning programs. What compelled you to stick around? What made you care and why? If you can build emotional hooks into your programs, the people will thank you.

chapter 6

Interactivity That Counts

In this chapter . . .

- Why does adding more clicks to your program not make it more interactive?

- What are the dangers of clicky-clicky bling-bling and what can you do to avoid it?

- What are four simple things you can do to create learning programs with more inner-bling?

No matter what tool your e-learning program will be developed in, chances are you've heard from key stakeholders and subject matter experts that they really just want to make sure that it's "engaging and interactive." Do you know what they mean? Do they know?

In the stakeholder's mind "make it interactive" often means "create me a cute little PowerPoint presentation that users interact with by clicking "next" to move to the next screen, add some onscreen clicks to explore content, and then throw in a few multiple choice questions for real impact."

On the other hand, "make it interactive" could also mean "design a fully immersive learning experience where the learner interacts with the user interface to make key decisions, sees the consequences of their choices, and decides the color of their avatar's hair. But we have a really tight budget, OK?"

When our customers and stakeholders and managers tell us, as e-learning designers, to make our programs interactive they have their reasons. Maybe they've heard other people use the term *interactive* and they like the sound of it. If it sounds like a game, maybe it will be a more interesting experience. Maybe they think it will make the program more fun and engaging. Or, maybe they just think it will help people learn better. Interactive programs may very well do all of these things, but not always.

Although clicking a "next" button technically denotes *interaction*, this is not the type of interactivity that people aim for when they talk about creating "more engaged learners." Interactivity is about what happens *in between* all those "next" buttons.

So what is interactivity, really?

Interaction
When Things Work Together

Doctors concern themselves with how different drugs will interact inside their patients' bodies. They want to know what happens when the chemicals meet. Will good stuff happen or nasty side effects? Our bodies move due to a complex series of interactions between our neurons, muscles, bones, tendons, ligaments and more. Signals and chemicals trigger reactions in cells that generate movement. When things have an effect or influence on something else, they are interacting.

Break it down: inter + act. When things act with or on each other, they are interconnected.

When We Make Things Happen

When we interact with an object or a device we typically expect a reaction. In human-computer terms that means you touch it and something happens—there are inputs and outputs.

Have you ever played with a static electricity lamp? A static electricity lamp is one of those glass balls with electric arcs that zap around the inside. When you touch its surface, the current moves to you and it's like lightening is coming out of your hands. It's a really cool reaction from an inanimate object, right? Kids love them and so do I.

Back in the olden days we would stick our finger in a rotary dial and spin it around a bunch of times to make a phone call. Magic, right? The phone started ringing at the other end.

When humans interact with machines, we make things happen. Computers turn on at the press of a button (usually), fans whir into action, dishwashers start washing when we switch them on, words miraculously appear on my monitor as I bang these words into my keyboard. We interact with machines and devices all day long without even thinking about it most of the time. And we expect these machines and devices to respond to our input and perform the expected behaviors. Most of the time, they do (otherwise, we start cursing and kicking).

The user interface of the computer or the machine influences how we interact with it. A well-designed user interface will make for an easy-to-use and intuitive produce, whereas a poorly designed user interface can lead to confusion, frustration, and potentially disaster.

When We Communicate With Other Human Beings

Human to human communication is my favorite kind of interaction. When two people interact with each other they talk, they laugh, they yell, they clean the kitchen, they solve problems, they challenge each other to duels, they share, they learn. Even when they disown each other and never speak again, there's some level of interaction happening.

We are social creatures in relationship with each other. It's all about interactivity. No technology needed. This social interaction is at the heart of our world and it's something that a lot of people neglect in online learning experiences.

The Spectrum of Interactive Control

We consume and interact with technology inputs every day along a spectrum. At one end of the spectrum lies passive activity, at the other end total user control and freedom.

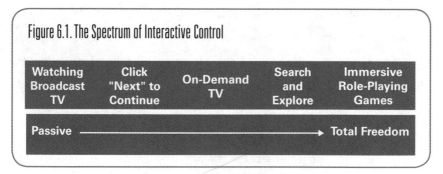

Figure 6.1. The Spectrum of Interactive Control

| Watching Broadcast TV | Click "Next" to Continue | On-Demand TV | Search and Explore | Immersive Role-Playing Games |

Passive ——————————————→ Total Freedom

Passive Viewing

Take your old fashioned TV-viewing experience. In the pre-Netflix and on-demand world, we would sit in front of our TVs and take what the networks gave us. Occasionally we might have changed the chan-nel. But mostly, we sat back and soaked it in—from entertainment to educational programming.

This is generally still true today: we watch the program without influ-encing it, although this is definitely changing. Through Twitter and Face-book, we share our thoughts in the moment about shows as they happen. Audience voting in reality singing or dancing competitions gives the audi-ence direct influence over the action, while other shows allow fans to influ-ence the plot lines of dramas and whether a TV show is cancelled.

Although passive viewing experiences are not interactive because we don't influence them or click on anything, we can still learn from them. I have learned quite a bit from wonderfully produced documentaries. Al Gore's *An Inconvenient Truth*, for example, got me hanging up laundry on the line on a more regular basis. Although I passively watched it, I actively changed my behavior as a result of viewing that program. I interacted with the content in my own mind. And I didn't click a thing, except the "on" button. This is powerful stuff, and we'll come back to it a little later in this chapter.

Search and Discover

Further along the spectrum from passive consumption lives the "search" world. TV and media viewing has become much less passive today due to on-demand options, digital recording devices, and the Internet. We now seek out what we want to consume by typing in a few keywords and clicking the magical search button. We browse and discover and surf—hours and hours at a time, even. We interact with systems to pull what we need and want to us.

Do you have a sheet of plywood and want to learn how to make a piece of furniture out of it? You could be like my husband and start searching, watch a video, check out some photos, read some reviews, and then download a plan. Later that afternoon, find yourself sitting in your new $17 plywood couch.

Are you a new manager and not sure how to have that difficult conversation with Brad, your 20-something employee? Start searching, read some articles, watch a few videos, click on a few links, and then write down what you want to say on a sticky note. Later that afternoon, find yourself having a productive conversation with Brad.

Through search and discovery you can find all sorts of resources. (And hopefully you have good critical thinking skills to discern what's useful and what's junk!) It's do-it-yourself (DIY) learning and it's what a lot of your employees are doing already. So how can you help them find what they need? Can you anticipate their needs and get the information out there that will be useful in bits and pieces?

Total Immersion and Influence

At the farthest end of the spectrum of interactivity sits a fully immersive and open world. In games like *World of Warcraft* and *Skyrim*, you select and design your own character, move through the world at will, team up with other players, and make choices on behalf of your character and how he should interact with the world. It's totally interactive and open. You can move where you want, in any direction that you want.

In the training world, think flight simulators or virtual environments, where you can role play a disaster response. For more on designing immersive environments, you might want to check out Koreen Olbrish Pagano's book, *Immersive Learning*.

Avoiding the Trap of Clicky-Clicky Bling-Bling

No matter where you're aiming for on the interactive spectrum, let's just be sure that you're not just throwing in a bunch of interactivity and clicking for interactivity's sake. I have a term for gratuitous interactivity and flashing bells and whistles: "clicky-clicky bling-bling" (CCBB). It's a sparkly term, isn't it? But also something you should really try to avoid.

So what is clicky-clicky bling-bling? It's e-learning with lots of whiz, lots of bang, lots of clicky-clicky in a lame attempt to add pizzazz to dry content and to make it more engaging. Once you unwrap the sparkle, sadly, all you're left with is a load of e-learning junk. Just because your e-learning sparkles and shimmers and gets the learner clicking on lots of fancy hotspots and has them dragging things all over the screen does not mean that you have engaged the learner.

So think about e-learning you've met in a dark room on a dull day. Was there any clicky-clicky bling-bling lurking on your screen?

- Perhaps it looked like a really fun learning game, but turned out to be a multiple-choice quiz in the form of a board game or nine holes of golf. *Kind of boring, right? And what does golf have to do with your day job?*

- Maybe the graphics sparkled and flashed and captured your attention. *Might be pretty, but in the end of the interface was so convoluted that you had no idea what to do and eventually gave up.*

- Could be there was a glorious and flashing "next" button that took over your field of vision. *Instead of paying attention to all of that so-called meaningful content, you were drawn like a moth to flame and just had to click that pretty, blinking "next" button.*

- Possibly what you saw before you was the most realistic representation of your new organization's campus. Every building had a clickable hot spot allowing you to dive in and more deeply explore what your company does. It's exciting! So much to learn! *But there are 32 things to click on and it's only noon and . . . wow, are you hungry.*

Exhaustion and fatigue sets in and you forget to return.

You've seen these programs. Admit it. And quite possibly, you have even helped to build them.

In the name of trying to make e-learning that looks good, provides interactive experiences, and will engage people, we may fall prey to what Ruth Clark and Richard Mayer, in *e-Learning and the Science of Instruction*, call "seductive details."

Sounds pretty intriguing, doesn't it? But isn't this a family show? Aren't we all about corporate learning? Doesn't seduction imply some horrible breach of the "company behavior in the workplace" policy? It reminds me of that story I heard once about the president of company I worked at many years ago. And, well, you can just imagine. It involved a lot of water cooler gossip and raised eyebrows, but there was never any proof. . . .

Did you see what I did just there? I took you down a slightly irrelevant path, didn't I? I seduced you to pay attention to my little sidebar rant that doesn't really pertain to interactivity, the supposed point of this chapter. I spiced things up a bit, while distracting you from the more important work of this chapter. And therein lies the definition!

Seductive details are "interesting but irrelevant material added to a multimedia presentation in an effort to spice it up" (Clark and Mayer 2007, 115).

As instructional designers, even if we're here by accident, we should know better, right? We should know that we need to stay on point and focused. So why does clicky-clicky bling-bling keep on happening? Clark and Mayer tell us:

> Consumers may feel that a "jazzier" product will hold the learner's inter-
> est better. This is the premise underlying the arousal theory, the idea that
> entertaining and interesting embedded effects cause learners to become
> more emotionally aroused and therefore they work harder to learn the
> material. (2007, 117)

Earlier in this chapter, I mentioned some of the reasons why our clients want interactive e-learning. Making it fun and engaging float to the top of that list almost every time. Stakeholders and designers alike get caught up in the glamour of it all, equating games and interactivity as ways to make learning more fun, and thus more effective.

The marketplace today is filled with rapid e-learning authoring tools and a wide selection of easy to use templates that make it a snap for novice developers to create game shows or interactive exercises with lots of clicky-clicky bling-bling. But just because it's easy, doesn't mean we should do it.

As I've said before, I'm all for templates as a way to streamline develop-ment, provide a solid toolkit for the learning designer, and give the learner a consistent but varied experience. But beware of templates that just spew forth more clicky-clicky bling-bling into the universe. If you're coming up with your own template set, design with care. If you're buying off-the-shelf templates, please buy with caution!

But let's not blame all CCBB on the tools. Let's also blame ourselves. As instructional designers and e-learning developers we need to understand the basics of effective instructional design and refrain from committing instructional design malpractice.

Kevin Thorn with Nuggethead Studioz, blames the deluge of CCBB on a lack of real design skills. He says people are "hiding content behind CCBB because there's no real design (instructionally or otherwise)."

Maybe it's easier to pay attention to the sparkle on the outside of the package rather than the value of the gift inside.

The Bright Side of Bling

Bling does indeed sparkle and shine, and it does have a bright side.

In fact, a bit of bling may help to motivate some learners. Extrinsic motivation comes from outside us, in the form of rewards (think points and badges), whereas intrinsic motivation comes from within, from an inner desire to learn and achieve mastery without the need for those external rewards.

Simple quiz games may help learners stick with the program and can help if you are testing declarative knowledge—facts and information that you want the learner to memorize. You may be familiar with the term "drill and kill"—drill them until they can't see straight and maybe they'll remember it!

Games and immersive experiences can provide arenas for deep exploration of a concept and lots of opportunity for effective practice—when done right. And even a drill and kill style multiple choice quiz may have its place in the world. Imagine a "Climb the Mountain Quiz Game" where each correct answer puts your onscreen character another point closer to climbing a tall mountain. If the "reward" of seeing your character reach the top of the mountain is sufficiently motivating, you might just stick around and finish that 30-question quiz. Maybe.

So there may be some value to this model, but more often than not these games turn into what Clark Quinn calls "tarted up" or "prettified drill and kill" (2013). The problem with this type of game is that it often provides no relevance to the real world in which your learners operate. I don't see many people in my target audience groups who actually climb mountains for a living, do you? And who aside from Pat Sajak and Alex Trebeck plays a game show for their day job? When we force learners to practice without context, we may help them memorize facts in the moment, but that doesn't mean that they'll be able to pull those facts out in the correct context at the moment of need.

Another fundamental problem with a lot of these game templates is that the questions that people write for them are often so terrible. In *Gadgets, Games and Gizmos for Learning* (2007), Karl Kapp, professor of instructional design and technology at Bloomsburg University, makes an argument for casual games as a keystone of learning, but reminds us that we need to write good questions first: "Well-written multiple choice-questions teach and assess knowledge within the context of a game. Poor questions simply allow the gamer to play the game without learning. Work to develop effective questions to force learning and require learners to think as they play the game" (71).

Sebastian Deterding, researcher, designer, and proponent of "gameful design," calls the nine-hole golf course quiz type of game a "disconnected challenge" (2013). Meaning, the challenge of the game has no connection to the reality in which the individual works and lives.

Deterding also points out that games are fun when they are voluntary. We have fun when we opt in and have the autonomy to choose. Games that the corporation forces on its poor employees? Not fun. Not fun at all. In fact, they are often annoying and highly mocked by the people who are subjected to them.

When done well, learning games are fun and great and actually help people learn. But when done poorly, they can so easily go bad.

Distracting to the Learner

Will Thalheimer analyzed research about the "seductive-details effect" from the late 1980s and 1990s, which found "that the addition of interesting yet unimportant augmentations can divert learners from learning the main points that are being made" (2004, 5).

The same argument could be made about the flamboyant classroom instructor who inspires and excites his students, earning rave reviews, but fails to inspire any lasting behavioral change in the learners or impart any lasting knowledge. Do you know this teacher? He tells amazing stories about the balloon delivery man dressed as an ape who actually slipped on a banana peel while getting onto an elevator. That lunch he had last week at that new restaurant downtown? Highly memorable and you're going there because of his recommendation. But did you actually retain any of the information he shared with you? Do you think you can do that new process he showed you next month when you need to do it again? Hmmm, yeah maybe that stuff didn't stick. Sounds like his performance mattered more than yours.

Exciting stories and glamour can make a course more engaging, but they may cause you to miss the point entirely. David Merrill, in "First Principles of Instruction," writes that "Graphics, animation, and other presentation enhancements are often used with the intent of increasing learner motivation. While these devices can attract a learner's attention, they are usually insufficient for sustaining attention over an extended period of time. Too often such devices become tiring and actually interfere with effective learning" (2009, 21).

Tom Kuhlmann, vice president of community at Articulate, writes The Rapid E-Learning Blog, which is a must read for any instructional designer—accidental or otherwise. In his December 1, 2009, post he goes on about designers who add background audio to an otherwise really boring course. "Guess what? If the course is boring, adding audio will only make it boring and danceable. You're best served to spend your time designing the right type of course and spending less time looking for ways to 'jazz it up.'"

When distractions abound, we miss the important things. And so do our students. Clicky-clicky bling-bling distracts the learner and doesn't promote deeper understanding. So, we put out a lot of effort to design this masterpiece, with no return.

The other real negative to clicky-clicky bling-bling is all that clicking. Have you ever gotten click fatigue on a desktop-based learning program? Twelve hotspots to click on this screen, followed by eight draggable items that exploded into the bin with fireworks when you dragged them to the correct location, followed by 42 pages of clicking the "next" button. It's exhausting just writing that.

And the fatigue is not just finger-clicking fatigue. It's ennui and boredom and mental fatigue—"Really, there's more? Please, someone release me!"

So How Can You Tell If It's Seductive and Distracting?

Aside from your e-learning program showing up late at night at your house wearing a black tuxedo and holding a rose between its teeth, how will you know if it's seductive and distracting?

First of all, be sure to look at it with a beginner's mind. Pretend that you've never looked at this program before, even if it's all you've thought about for the last three weeks. Do a visual scan and run through it with a pair of slightly glazed over eyes. (This may not be hard if you've been working all day.) Squint your eyes and look at an individual page. Where does your eye naturally land? If it immediately goes to the softly pulsing next button in the bottom right corner, then you may have a problem. Does your eye miss all the important content and simply stick to the lovely animation of the soda cans spilling all over the supermarket floor? Yeah, you may need to fix something.

Do some pilot testing. Put the course in front of a few crash test dummies—ideally, real people within your organization, but your friends and family could also work. Usability testing and focus groups can help you uncover problems like hard-to-use navigation, overwhelming screens, or just plain dull design. The opposite of clicky-clicky bling-bling is surely clicky-clicky blah blah so be on guard for both!

Once the material is released into the wild, follow up with people who have taken the program—those who completed the whole thing, as well as those who never got through it. Use surveys or in-person conversations and take the time to check in with people immediately afterward, then again in a few weeks. Find out what stuck with them at the end of the program. See what they remembered and, more importantly, what they could actually apply or do. If all they remember is the catchy tune from the course opening, then you know you've got a problem.

This guidance really applies to any program, not just as a test for CCBB.

Clicky-clicky bling-bling is the e-learning equivalent of adding more cowbell. Brandon Carson, an award-winning instructional designer, made a comment on his Facebook page about how adding gratuitous interactivity to e-learning is like adding more cowbell. And I have to agree. The cowbell reference comes from a *Saturday Night Live* sketch with Will Ferrell and Christopher Walken, which shows the band Blue Oyster Cult in the recording studio. Will Ferrell plays an earnest musician, really passionate about his cowbell. Walken, playing the role of the slick record producer, keeps stopping the band to urge, "we need more cowbell." By the end of the sketch, the cowbell has completely drowned out the rest of the song.

I have a yoga-teacher friend named Michelle who promotes the harmonious concept of inner bling. She exhorts us to shed our stuff, stop focusing on the material world, and let our inner bling shine through. Just like people, great e-learning designs can shine from the inside. They can have "inner bling" as opposed to clicky-clicky bling-bling. A learner will then remember what mattered about the e-learning program and not just the shiny wrapper.

So, what's the trick? Well, the best way to avoid clicky-clicky bling-bling—and it's actually not a trick at all—is to engage people's brains and actually make them think. Cognition is way more powerful than clicking.

A brain that interacts with the content reflects on the material to better integrate it into it's existing thought patterns and engages with the material through practice and relevant activity. Now that's interactivity that counts.

Less Clicking, More Thinking

Let's take a look next at four simple strategies you can incorporate into learning designs that are less about the clicking and more about the thinking: get them feeling, get them doing, get them reflecting, and get them connecting.

Get Them Feeling

The other night I was in a hotel room flipping through the TV channels. I don't remember what show was on, but there was a really great commercial for FaceTime on the iPhone. It featured all these emotional and human scenes of people connecting with their loved ones through their devices. I had just finished FaceTiming with to my five-year-old who was nervous because she was having a minor surgical procedure the next day. I was heartbroken that I wasn't there with her, and man, did this iPhone commercial cut right to that emotional core for me. I cried.

Even a passive experience like watching a commercial can cause a real emotional and physiological reaction in our bodies. That commercial tapped into my experience and caused a change in my breathing, temperature, and mood. If that's not interactive, then what is? That commercial had an effect on me and I felt connected to this tribe of people around the world who used their iPhones to FaceTime. Brand solidarity.

Marketing people know the power of emotion. As learning designers, we can harness this power by connecting with our audience at a human level. We can talk to them like people, stir up strong feelings through powerful stories, and help them see how this content matters to them. When we help people see the WIIFM (what's in it for me?) we help them make the connections between the computer screen and the everyday world where their performance matters.

Help them see why they should pay attention and maybe they will.

Hooking someone in with a strong emotion—through a powerful story, a shocking statistic, or a provocative question—creates cognitive sticky points, allowing the content to embed itself more deeply in the individual's mind.

Find ways to tell those powerful stories. Put the learner into the story, and make them sweat, if you can. Go back to chapter 5 for more ideas and strategies.

Get Them Doing

Of course, it's not interactive if we don't ever get people acting or doing. Through application and practice we promote learning and skill development so that people can go back to their day jobs and just do it.

E-learning can be the dress rehearsal for the real deal. Short of creating a truly immersive interactive role-playing environment, think of simple but effective ways that you can get the learner doing something in your online learning programs. During the initial project analysis one of your first tasks was to identify what you wanted the learner to be able to do with the information you are sharing with them. Right? You do this already. You might call this process "identifying the learning objectives." Instead, let's think in terms of identifying "performance outcomes."

But rather than spend too much time obsessing over which verb from Bloom's Taxonomy you're going to use for each of your learning objectives, spend that time with your subject matter expert and key stakeholders to find out what they really want people be able to do at the end of the day. Once you have identified that, you can figure out how to help people practice those skills.

Provide Relevant Practice

Make sure that what you have them do is relevant to their situation. Those quizzes in the form of a mountain climbing achievement? That's disconnected challenge. Be sure to create a connected challenge that maps back to the reality of the learner's world. By creating relevance and context, you create retrieval hooks that let him pull that information off the shelf when he needs it.

A few years ago, a major hair care company hired us to create an online program for their national educators—professional stylists who go into other salons and educate other stylists about the company's products. They are classic SMEs turned trainers; their specialty is hair care, not education or training.

The goal of the program we designed was to teach the national educators about the company's new product line so that they could go into salons, get the stylists to use the products effectively to delight their customers, and, ultimately, drive up product sales. Because it turns out that if you don't understand how color products affect hair structure you could turn someone's dark hair orange if you're trying to lighten it. (Learning stuff like this is why I love my job!)

The online learning program, as part of a blended curriculum, served as the prework for classroom sessions and role-playing activities. Although we had a limited budget, we still wanted to give them the opportunity to practice what they had learned. But we didn't just want to subject them to drill-and-kill style questions. Instead, we created a series of multiple-choice questions that were phrased as if a stylist in the salon were asking them. We put context around the questions and made it feel more like the environment in which they would be asked to recall the information. It's a simple thing that makes a big difference in preparing people to do what they need to do.

Goal-Based Scenarios

Another way to get people doing and provide context and relevant practice is through goal-based scenarios. In a goal-based scenario, you drop the learner into a scene and put her in charge of what happens. You set up the situation, give her a challenge or problem, and then provide choices and decisions along the way that direct the outcome. Tom Kuhlmann calls this the three Cs: challenge, choice, and consequence.

So, instead of opening the program with the standard screen after screen of content and information, the first page puts the learner right into a realistic situation. "You are the isolations specialist on a new oil rig and need to complete your initial task analysis."

The overall point of the learning program is to achieve the goal—in this case to complete an initial task analysis. As the scene unfolds, ask her what she should do first, by building a text screen and graphic screen followed by a multiple choice question. The templates that you use here don't have to be fancy; it's really all in the story. The learner may already know the information necessary to answer the question correctly (and move on to the next stage of the story). If not, provide supplemental resources and information that she can dig into more deeply to get the knowledge she'll need in order to answer the question.

A goal-based scenario can be a great tool for practicing complex problem-solving skills. Through sidebars and resources buttons, you can provide access to supporting documents and job aids that will help inform the decision-making process and give the learner hands-on experience using real resources to solve real problems.

There are various levels of complexity for a goal-based senario that can involve full-on branching exercises in the choose-your-own-adventure style, or you can design a simpler version—what I call "fake branching." You can read more about goal-based scenarios and fake branching in chapter 4.

Create an Action Plan

Another idea to get people doing things in your learning program is to have them create their own action plans. As the course progresses, have them fill out fields in an onscreen form, download and complete a Word document, or simply have them write down their actions on a piece of paper. At the end of the exercise, they will have listed the steps they need to take.

For example, in a sales program they might have to identify three leads to follow through with next week, two products to take for a spin, and one topic to discuss with their manager in the next sales review call. Action plans and worksheets create forward momentum and provide people with something real and tangible to take away from the online learning program.

Get Them Reflecting

If having a conversation with another human being is an interactive activity, then so is having a conversation with yourself. Reflection is cognitive interactivity—things happening inside the brain as you move ideas around and figure out just where you're going to put new information.

Reflecting on our experiences and what we have learned provides us with an opportunity to incorporate new knowledge into our existing mental models.

This is what David Merrill, in "First Principles of Instruction," calls the integration principle. He says that, "an opportunity for meaningful reflection increases the probability that the skill will be retained and used in the every-day lives of the learners" (2009, 20). Merrill then goes on to talk about reflection and integration as happening in discussions with teachers and peers, but there are also ways to encourage reflection in a self-paced program.

A simple way to build a reflective moment is to just stop and ask a question, no clicking required. Build a pause into the program to get the learner to stop and think. This can be a simple text and graphic screen that asks a thoughtful question like, "Think about a course you are designing right now. Could you incorporate a reflective question screen in the course flow? Why or why not?"

Invite the learner to take notes along the way. In fact, why don't you do that right now? In this book or on a piece of paper, write down one way that you could use a reflective pause in your next program. If pencils and pens seem too old-fashioned, you could have the learner complete an online worksheet or journal. Or, if you'd like to stick to the on-screen activity, provide text input screens where the participant can actually type out their thoughts and ideas. Most of the off-the-shelf e-learning authoring tools have an open input screen type, so this isn't a daunting technological task.

You can also use slider bars, Likert scales (on a scale of 1-5), and even multiple choice questions to ask people to rate themselves. Ask questions like, "How confident are you about talking to teenagers one-one-one?" and "On a scale of one to five, how ready to you feel to start doing Z tomorrow?"

If the learner takes the time to complete the exercise, that's great. And if all they do is stop and look at the screen and consider the question, well, that's also great. You've still created a reflective moment in the action, allowing the learner to internalize the content and integrate it into their own way of thinking.

As you consider adding reflective moments to a self-paced program, here are some questions you can ask:

- What do you think about . . . ?
- How are you doing this now . . . ?
- Did you notice . . . ?
- How can you improve in this area?
- Why did that happen?
- How can you use that?
- How confident are you about . . . ?

Get Them Connecting

Even though you focus on creating technology-based learning programs, don't forget about human-to-human communication. Remember that? It's my favorite form of interactivity, but maybe that's to be expected, given that I'm a bit of an extrovert. Human connection is primal and basic. We learn from each other by sharing our experiences, bouncing ideas off each other, and working through problems. Even for noted introverts, human connection plays a key part in learning.

Back to Merrill's "First Principles of Instruction":

> When instruction provides an opportunity for learners to discuss what they have learned with other students or to defend what they have learned when challenged, then they are put in the role of teacher. Meaningful discussion and the need to defend one's skills requires the kind of deep reflection that enables learners to refine their mental models, to eliminate misconceptions, and to increase the flexibility with which they use their new skill.

[handwritten margin note: high level Bloom, w/out formal instruction]

How can we find ways to build human connection into our learning designs? How can you take the program beyond e-learning and into the realm of social interaction?

Social networking and collaborative tools in the workplace make this process easier than ever before. Find ways to make use of social business tools already in use at your organization (like Yammer or Jive) to unlock your content from the computer and take it into the realm of human conversation. If your organization allows it, take advantage of tools and platforms where the people already spend their time, like Facebook and Twitter. Facebook has pages and groups that you can make secret and by invitation only. These sites provide a rich platform for creating ongoing conversation and connection around training topics and providing a forum where people can problem solve and share crucial information to getting the job done. Jane Bozarth's *Social Media for Trainers* provides a lot of ideas and insights into using social tools to enhance traditional training.

But don't assume that your solution needs to be technology driven. What if you found a way to get real people sitting down and talking to other real people face-to-face? What a glorious day it would be, wouldn't it? We've already talked about ways to take learning beyond the course using note-taking, action plans, and worksheets. What if you use those as prompts for real, live conversations? *idea for PML ?*

With that in mind, include a downloadable, printable worksheet that the learner fills out as he goes along. This could be as simple as a link to a word document; it does not need to be something fancy that you have to program or attach to a database. This word document serves as a repository for questions, reflective moments, and action items that the learner can review and discuss with his manager. It could be a great add-on to a leadership program or other soft skills topic.

You can also make use of survey tools to prompt that human connection. At the end of the program include a link to a short survey that will be sent to the participant's manager. Ask three questions that could spark a conversation about the subject matter, such as "What did you notice about . . . ?" or "How will you apply that to your job role?" or "How can you use that in your own day-to-day workflow?"

Most learning management systems allow you to set up rules and triggers to prompt a human connection. As part of a blended leadership program we created for a global manufacturing program, the manager and the employee had to sit down and have a discussion about the program. The next section of the learning program only appeared when the manager signed off on that conversation in the LMS. While this kind of gated checkpoint may feel restrictive to your autonomy as a learner, it provides structure and guidance through the learning program with regular opportunity for coaching and feedback.

Of course, any type of human-to-human communication will only be as good as the people involved. So, if the people are difficult, then you may have bigger problems on your hands!

Make the Interaction Count!

In the name of creating something engaging and sticky, stakeholders urge us to create interactivity. But, more often than not, it just ends up being lots of meaningless clicking. And let's be real, nobody likes pointless clicking or silly exercises that represent completely disconnected challenges to the work that we need to do. Too much clicking and too many seductive details leads to learner fatigue, distracts the learner, and doesn't promote deeper understanding.

So, instead of filling up your online learning programs with distracting clicky-clicky bling-bling, find ways to promote cognitive interactivity through techniques that drum up the emotional response and get people doing, reflecting, and connecting.

chapter 7

Writing Better E-Learning

In this chapter . . .

- How can you write e-learning programs that don't bore people to tears?

- What key principles can you follow for better scripting?

- How can you convince stakeholders to lighten up so you can create something more accessible?

Good writing is the single biggest factor that can make the difference between an e-learning program that bores people to death and one that gets them to pay attention. It's all in the delivery and how you present the information. Far too often, e-learning designers take the CBT Lady approach, loading page after page with text bullet after text bullet.

Let's imagine a compliance training program in your organization. The topic? Rules and regulations for speaking at trade shows. This 10-page policy document is so boring that no one actually reads it. So, now the stakeholders want to make it mandatory e-learning. The CBT Lady gets to work and here's what she comes up with:

The first screen of the e-learning says that the program has audio in it and to be sure to use your headset. You click "next." Now you hear three minutes of audio narration explaining how to use the buttons in the course. Next! Then come the dreaded learning objectives—"At the end of this course, you will have learned . . ."—followed by 15 bullets of poorly written blah, blah, blah. Yeah, whatever. Next! Finally, the content actually describing the policy appears! But it's three paragraphs of on-screen text with audio narration; content copied directly from a policy document that a lawyer wrote and no one can actually understand.

This goes on for 12 more screens. The CBT Lady was thoughtful enough to include a short scenario so you can see the policy in action. That's one screen of the course and not so bad. After that comes a 15-question quiz filled with true/false questions. If you get more than three questions wrong, the buzzer sounds and you have to retake the quiz to get a completion status in your learning management system.

It's enough to make you want to gouge your eyes out in despair. It's the stuff of nightmares, and the type of e-learning program that gives all other e-learning programs a bad name. Boring. Boring. Boring. Clicky-clicky blah-blah.

I spoke with a client just last week who works in regulatory affairs at a pharmaceutical company. She told me that so much of what their employees deal with every day is paperwork, jargon, and dense legalese. "These people are already buried in boring," she explained. "We need to make something stand out from all of that."

There are lots of ways to make e-learning that stands out, from better visual design, to relevant interactivity, and a good overall hook. In my mind, however, the first and foremost rule to better e-learning is better writing.

When I started at Kineo in 2009, one of the first lessons I had on writing better e-learning came from Stephen Walsh. Stephen, a Kineo co-founder, hails from Ireland, has written a play or two, and can make a boring e-learning program sing. He knows his writing.

Stephen laid out Kineo's framework for writing better e-learning programs. In my early days at Kineo, I had the pleasure of running a joint webinar with Kirstie Greany, one of our senior learning consultants. Maybe it's that British thing they both have going on, but they both know how to add snap and crackle to a script. I've modified Stephen's original list for my purposes and have added a few more over the years, but the principles stand true no matter what you call them: make it human, keep it light, cut it out, give it spirit, treat them like grown-ups, find your flow, and be on brand. We try to sprinkle this special fairy dust over every project we do. These principles help you find the right tone so you can turn your work from clicky-clicky blah-blah to something with a lot more oomph.

Make It Human

My mantra for e-learning is, "It's all about the people, man." When we write passive scripts that are full of jargon and abstract, impersonal language, we completely neglect to connect with the person sitting on the other end of that computer. If there's only one thing you do differently in your e-learning designs, let this be it: make it human. Talk to people. Connect with them. Make the e-learning sound like it's a conversation between people. Real people; not robots.

Instead of saying:

> "In order to effectively manage employee performance, managers need to successfully navigate difficult conversations with their employees. In this e-learning program, you will learn three techniques you can apply to employee conversations . . ."

Try this:

> "Have you ever had a difficult conversation with one of your employees? Where did you struggle and why? In this short program, we're going to explore three things you can do to make those conversations less difficult and more productive. Sound good?"

When you speak directly to the learner, you're making use of the personalization principle, which is when you have a conversation directly with someone using first and second person language like "we" and "you." Ruth Clark and Richard Mayer (2003) tell us that using the personalization principle actually yields better learning results than more formal language.

When I urge you, my dear reader, to try this writing style in your next e-learning program, do you feel a little more compelled to consider the approach? Do you feel like I'm asking you for a personal favor and that you might let me down if you ignore it? Because you will. You will let me down, as well as the people who will be subjected to your otherwise impersonal e-learning scripts.

Make it human. Talk to the people.

Keep It Light

What conversations do you enjoy more? The kind that are dense, heavy, and serious in tone? Or short, snappy, with a little bit of humor thrown in? Do you like a lecture thrown at you or a conversation with you? Even when the content is serious, giving it a bit of levity makes it more accessible and human.

This may be my personal style, but I've found that most people prefer the lighter touch. It's how normal human beings talk to each other in normal conversation. Unless, of course, we're being lectured at by some stiff-lipped professorial type who is lost in his academic tomes or a prim corporate lawyer full of legalese and regulatory mumbo jumbo. But that treads very quickly into the land of glazed eyes, drooling lips, and nodding heads. Let's spare our learners from that unique form of suffering, OK? As best as you can, try to lighten up.

Instead of:

> "This e-learning course is designed to explain the 15 steps needed to complete our regulatory process . . ."

Why not try this?

> "Need to get your head around our process? We all do! So let's take a look at the 15 steps."

This second approach sounds more human. It's the conversational tone that we talked about already, but it's also go a lighter touch, sounds more fun and inviting, and overall has just a touch more sass. I like sass.

But going lighter isn't just about turning up the sass volume. A lighter touch uses simpler language, which means less cognitive overhead for your audience. If you have to spend a lot of effort deciphering every other big word, you're not going to absorb as much of the critical information that really matters. So while you're keeping it light, drop the jargon and drop the big words.

In *Made to Stick*, Chip Heath and Dan Heath remind us that, "Language is often abstract, but life is not abstract" (2008, 99). When we use obtuse, abstract language, we make it harder for people to understand and remember what we're saying. Abstract jargon belongs to the experts. Keeping your language concrete, especially for novices, helps people better grasp new concepts.

How can you take it down a notch? Explain abstract concepts by putting the focus on things that are concrete and familiar—put relevant context around the concepts to help people organize this new information into their existing mental models or "schemas." This ties back to Robert Gagné's third event in the Nine Events of Instruction: stimulate recall of prior knowledge. By using familiar language and tying it back to the terminology and ideas that people already know, you're building a stronger learning experience.

It's one thing to avoid the jargon of the subject matter expert, but you also need to take care to avoid the jargon of instructional design. I talked about this more in chapter 5, but the bottom line is spare people from having to suffer through bulleted lists of learning objectives.

To be clear here, keeping it light doesn't mean unprofessional or flippant, and you certainly have control over how light you go.

Corporations and serious-minded stakeholders may object to a lighter tone. Have you ever had someone tell you that their content was serious stuff and should be treated that way? I have. These are people who think their content is serious and important and, therefore, should not be taken lightly. Ever. They might be right, to some degree. But they also seem to think that the more fancy, pretentious words they use, the more seriously other people will take it.

I would certainly not suggest writing a course about protecting children in emergencies in a humorous and joking tone. But perhaps a program on the financial implications of a regulatory disaster could stand a little levity. You do need to use your best judgment on the humor part. But certainly talking in a conversational and human approach works better every time.

Your challenge, should you choose to accept it: convince these serious-minded stakeholders otherwise. Show them, through example, how people prefer a lighter style over a stiffer, more serious tone. Try building a few screens of a course in two different ways and getting their input. Ask them, "Which would you prefer?" Better yet, take those sample screens in front of some real people who would actually be the recipients of this learning program and ask them, "Which would you prefer?" Collect the data and take the proof back to the stakeholders.

There are additional challenges with this, especially with a global audience. You need to be careful that short and snappy doesn't translate into colloquial slang that no one in East Nagwali will understand.

Cut It Out

This one goes without saying: cut, cut, cut. Less really is more. Cut your scripts. Get to the point quickly and spare the learner endless screens with endless text.

In a slide-based e-learning program, try aiming for one idea per slide, instead of cramming in 14 ideas on one slide just because you can get the font that small. People need mental and visual space to consider and consolidate an idea. Give it to them in simple, easily digestible chunks. And then cut it some more.

Give It Spirit — active voice (check scripts for)

We all know by now that to be a good writer the words you write need to be written in an active and not a passive voice.

Hey, look at that. I just used the passive voice. Kind of boring.

Instead of making "you" (the noun) the object of that sentence, I made it the subject. You can spot the passive voice by the use of the words "to be" or "is."

I find it hard to write in an active voice. It's much easier to write passively and sometimes just takes too much time to find that exciting and spirited twist to give a certain sentence a special oomph. But passive is boring and it is without energy and it is without an active participant. See? I keep doing it!

Writing in an active voice may take more time and you'll need creativity, energy, and patience. But you know what? It makes for a more energetic and engaging experience for the person on the receiving end. An active voice invites us in, makes us part of the action, and inspires action and participation.

Finding that spirit takes more than an active voice. You need to make it an invitation, and give it a special something that makes people want to participate in your program, that makes them really want to click "next."

This?	Or this?
"The fabulous e-learning script was written by you."	"You wrote the fabulous e-learning script."
"The process briefing document is used to define our core requirements."	"The process briefing document defines our core requirements."
"Now that you have covered the basics of customer service, in the next section you will learn how to deal with customer issues."	"You're one step away from maximizing your skills, but there's a problem—a customer one in fact. Click 'next' to put your skills to the test."

I like column two. What about you?

Giving it spirit doesn't really mean that you need to pull out your pom-poms and create false cheer, but spirited language that invites and inspires is a simple way to pump up the volume, find your active voice, and pull people in.

Treat Them Like Grown-Ups

I have seen far too many e-learning programs that patronize people, talk down to them, and essentially assume that they are idiots. Learners are busy professionals—treat them like that and give them the respect they deserve. The tone of voice you use to write the program should sound like an adult speaking to an adult, not a parent to a child. Give them choices and respect their time—and intelligence.

Do you really need to tell them on every single screen that the "next" button is in the bottom right corner? Don't you think they learned that when they had to click "next" on the very first screen?

What the e-learning screen says:	What the learner thinks:
"By now you have learned . . ."	"Oh, really? The truth is, I didn't learn a darn thing. Now who looks stupid? You or me?"
"You must do . . ."	"No. I don't have to *do* anything. You can't make me. You're not my mommy."
"This will take 90 minutes"	"Actually, I don't have 90 minutes. So instead I took 15 minutes because I just rushed through it and the final quiz was so easy I could have passed it without viewing any of your content pages. So don't tell me how long something is going to take! Or if you do, give me some choices."
"To advance to the next screen click the 'next' button in the bottom right corner of your screen."	"Umm, yeah. I know my way around computers and smartphones. In fact, I'm pretty savvy about this stuff, but you seem to think I'm an idiot."

What if instead of telling your learners what they must do, you try to sell them on why it will be a valuable use of their time? Think like an advertiser and find the appeal, create the desire, and get them to see the benefits of taking five minutes to do your program. Instead of saying, "In this section, you'll learn the three things you need to do to run an effective meeting," try "Take five minutes to find out how to run effective meetings."

Find Your Flow

All too often, an e-learning course goes from slide to slide with no thread to stitch it all together, no cohesion to connect the ideas and information. Slide three says, "These are the four steps to submit a TPA Report." Slide four says, "These are the risks of not submitting a TPA report." Slide five presents yet another fact farm. At the end of the day, it's just a big information dump.

You need to find your flow.

We've talked already about making e-learning sound like a conversation. Finding the flow is really just that—using simple techniques to make one slide build off the previous slide to connect ideas and show people how it all fits together. It's how we talk to each other and how we share ideas.

This could be as simple as saying, "We just looked at the steps to follow for submitting. But why does this even matter? And what are the risks if we don't do it right? Let's find out." Or, you could make the whole course a single narrative, told as a guided story or a "day-in-the-life" approach where you follow one character through a process from start to finish. Another possibility is giving the course a voice using an audio narrator or a narrator character who plays the role of a coach, trusted advisor, or more experienced peer. By using the first person narrative, the content naturally unfolds in conversation.

In chapter 8, I'll talk more about scenarios and stories.

Be on Brand

A company's brand is about more than the logo and color palette. A company has a culture and personality that should influence the tone of voice and language you use. It's not just about throwing in the right acronyms and the jargon of your business, although that can be a part of it. Do your company's brand values reflect fun and excitement? Does that spirit get through? Is your brand more conservative and formal? Well, then you may need to go that route—just remember to keep it conversational and human, even if it's a little more formal.

Learning activities allow employees to reflect and commit to changing their behavior as part of the learning process. So it's a prime opportunity to reinforce the brand and its values through using elements such as visual design, tone of voice, and behavior examples in case studies and scenarios.

Quick thought: What gives your e-learning personality? What type of tone do you have? Need help? Talk to your marketing team!

Hone Your Writing Skills

What makes a good writer? Most good writers would say, writing. Writing a lot. I do think that for some, good writing comes naturally. For others, it's a painfully learned art and skill. And for others, it may just be something they never get. You probably have some sense of where you fit into this schema. We won't dwell on it too long, but I encourage you to keep writing.

When I write, I hear the words in my head. This works especially well when drafting an e-learning audio script, but it also works well for written text. When you hear it aloud, you hear the tone of voice, whether or not it makes sense, and can really feel whether or not you've got a good flow. If you don't hear things in your head, take the time to read what you've written out loud to yourself. Go find a closet where no one can see you talking to your screen, or just ignore their crazy looks.

As you read your script out loud, keep your ears open and ask yourself:

- Does it sound natural?

- Does it sound like a human being said these things or a robot?

- Would you want to read this thing? Really? Would you want to have to sit through this e-learning program? Really? If yes, fabulous. If not, what can you change to make it more compelling, more sticky, more human?

- What can you cut? If something doesn't relate to your key points, get rid of it.

Get Inspired

Have you ever spent time on SlideShare? It is a website where you can upload PowerPoint presentations and share them with the world. When I speak at conferences I post my slides there so they can be viewed later. Companies post marketing decks and thought leaders post missives on this and that. When I've got the time, I like to explore the featured pages on SlideShare to see what's hot. And a good PowerPoint deck can be really good.

Nancy Duarte has perfected the art of the PowerPoint and taught us that we can do a lot with this medium both visually and structurally. Her book *slide:ology: The Art and Science of Creating Great Presentations* is a great resource. Cliff Atkinson's *Beyond Bullet Points* redefined how I approach creating presentations, through tight but well written headlines and a single idea per slide. Forget the long text bulleted lists on each slide.

Some Places to Look

- Check out SlideShare to see how top presenters distill key ideas down to a strong visual and a snappy sentence or headline.

- Take notice of the world around you—from news headlines to social media posts, what pulls you in and makes you want to learn something?

- Pay attention to marketing materials that strike your fancy. How did the marketing team convey that idea? How did they incite your desire? What can you emulate or reuse?

- Check out Cathy Moore's great presentation, "Dump the Drone," which is available at http://www.slideshare.net/CathyMoore /dump-the-drone-easy-steps-to-livelier-elearning. _blog?_

Even though a lot of e-learning is about more than presenting information and content, we can pull a lot of these principles into our e-learning scripts. So go forth and write great e-learning scripts!

chapter 8

It's All in the Story

In this chapter . . .

- Why do stories work? Why do we pay attention to them?

- How can we get the right stories out of our subject matter experts (SMEs)?

- How can we use stories in our e-learning programs?

We've all heard that storytelling enhances learning; and that sharing relevant examples helps both the expert and the novice forge connections with the content to ensure effective knowledge transfer. We've heard that flight simulators save lives, that practice makes perfect, and that we should show rather than tell.

The best classroom instructors know this instinctively—they pepper their sessions with stories and anecdotes that make the content relevant and alive. And yet building scenarios and simulations into online learning can feel intimidating. It takes time. And money. And fancy 3D worlds with blue-haired avatars. Or full-length videos with high-end Hollywood budgets, actors, scenes, lighting, and camera crews.

Scenarios can be all that, but they can also be something simpler.

Why Do Stories Work?

Before we get into techniques you can use, let's make the case for why stories work.

Humans are primed for stories. As mommies and daddies we tell our children stories at bedtime. For entertainment, we watch movies and read books and sit around campfires and water coolers and regale each other with tales from the trenches. Stories are not only fun, we also learn from them. Novels give insight into how other people think, providing models for how we act or relate to others. Aesop's' fables teach memorable lessons of morality. History teaches us lessons learned and not learned.

Think back to a fabulous live classroom experience you've had—maybe there was a really great teacher at the head of the room, or a dynamic and engaging presenter in a virtual classroom. Off the top of your head, you may not remember the steps or the concept the presenter taught, but rather the instructive story she shared: The guy who did it all wrong and made his computer explode; or the learning designer who forgot to do an up-front analysis and the tragic hilarity that ensued.

If the story was relevant to the content (and not a distractor or song and tap dance that merely entertained), then it provided some mental hooks for you back to the content. So in remembering the story, you start to remember the content. These details hit us on a visceral level—they stick deep in the memory. When done right, they help you to reconnect with the content (the steps, the process, the point). When done poorly, all you remember is the story.

Stories stick us with context and ooze with humanity. When we immerse ourselves in stories, we empathize with the characters, we visualize the scene, and we often put ourselves right into the action. As a learning vehicle, stories add context and details that make the content relevant and relatable.

Rather than just reciting the five steps to good customer service word for word, it's better to see those steps in action through the eyes of Alexandra, a seasoned customer service rep. While Alexandra knows the five key principles, she sometimes gets a bit lax. In this hilarious journey, we're going to show you the kinds of mistakes she made. The hope? That you'll avoid making those mistakes yourself somewhere down the line.

When we immerse ourselves in stories we slip into the skin of the characters—even if it's just for a few moments—as we see the world through their eyes and live out their actions in our own minds. It's why we empathize with the villain when we live the story through their own eyes—it's like we're mentally rehearsing how to be them.

In *Made to Stick* Chip and Dan Heath name stories as one of the six key things that make ideas "stick." Just by hearing Alexandra's story, you're putting yourself into her shoes and "rehearsing" the experience in your own mind. "Mental simulation is not as good as actually doing something," they write, "but it's the next best thing." They go on to explain that the right kind of story is a simulation: "Stories are like flight simulators for the brain" (2008, 213).

In a nutshell, hearing stories is the next best thing to being there. What stories do you find the most memorable? What things stick in your head?

Think about your own life. Do you remember more of the good things that have happened to you or do you dwell on the negative?

The thing I remember most about sixth grade was the girl I ditched so I that could hang out with the cool kids. She had been my best friend for a while, but then I started avoiding her and saying mean things about her to other kids. Her name was Tracey and I still feel ashamed about how I behaved. In truth, it sounds like the plot of a Judy Blume novel.

Chances are, this story will stick in your head now whenever you think about me. Why? Because we seem to remember the bad things about people we meet more than the good. And, in general, bad things get more thought and attention than good things (Baumeister, Bratslavsky, Finkenauer et al., 2001). It's why this story is always in the top of my memory banks, and why you might think about poor Tracey should you ever meet me in person.

There's probably a survival of the fittest thing going on here. Biologically, our mental antennae tune into these warning tales—to teach us which predators to stay away from, which partners to avoid as mates, which people might betray us, and so on. When you meet me, you might wonder if I'll turn on you, too, or if I'm really trustworthy and loyal.

A 2011 study at Northeastern University in Boston, explored the effect of gossip on our attention spans. Subjects were exposed to images associated with stories about different characters and situations—some were negative, some were positive. Then, using a special image viewer, they were shown two separate images—one for each eye—while brainwave activity was tracked. The images that generated the most brainwave activity and interest were linked to the negative stories—those gossipy tales of warning.

We learn from mistakes, our own as well as the mistakes of others. When deciding what stories to use in your e-learning programs, start there. Start with the mistakes and show the resulting terrible consequences. People will pay attention to your program as they put cognitive effort into processing the information you have shared with them. Why? Because they need to figure out why this happened so they can avoid making the same mistake themselves.

Think of it as using the power of gossip to instruct.

Finding the Right Stories

How do you find the right stories to share in your programs? How do you find the stories that instruct rather than merely entertain? And how do you get deep down to the heart of those mistakes and that "bad" stuff that we just said people will pay more attention to?

Finding the right stories starts with asking the right questions of your subject matter experts.

Oftentimes, I'm charged with the task of converting a client's existing classroom training into an online self-paced program. So what do they give me? Their text-ridden, 68-slide PowerPoint decks, which they lovingly pat, saying "it's all in there."

But it never is ALL there, is it? What they've given you is all of the *information* and none of the *stories* behind it.

During an initial design workshop with a client, I like to ask four questions to get at the right story angle to use: What mistakes do people typically make? What stories do you tell people to illustrate this concept? What questions do people ask you? Where are their gaps in understanding?

If given the opportunity, I love observing an instructor in action (this could be live or on a webinar). This lets me capture all of the extra bits that aren't on the bulleted slides. What questions are the students asking as the content emerges and where do they seem stuck? What questions am I asking as the content emerges? How does the instructor make it come alive? What examples does she share? What stories does he naturally tell?

If my SME wants to give me an information dump, I keep asking for more stories and examples. I type really fast, which comes in handy at times like these. I try to capture the language they use, the slang they inject, and the life they breathe into their content. I transcribe what they say (as much as possible). Then, I'll use the sentences, stories, and examples from that transcript as I create the script for my e-learning program. If you don't type quickly or find transcription too distracting, I highly recommend you record the conversations so you can capture the stories and the essence later. But no matter how you do it, be sure to capture the extra juicy stuff. That's where your primordial ooze for this content lies—and it's the key to making the content come alive.

Now that you've got your story ideas, how can you make them a part of your e-learning program without completely blowing the budget and timeline? Remember, we're not talking here about going hog wild with a three-camera, five-day video shoot, on location with a PA, a key grip, a gaffer, and all that jazz. We're talking simple and scalable—something you can do today, using the tools and skills you already have. Let's look at an example of one way you can build a story in your program.

Use Short Stories to Exemplify

This is a simple approach I use a lot, especially on a project with a more rapid development timeline. Instead of bulking out the course with page after page of boring content, let people see it in action. Start with your story. Keep it short, sharp, and relevant to the content. Don't add too many flourishes or details—this is training, not a Hollywood movie!

Above all, make sure the story is realistic—something that your learners will believe and identify with. So much of learning comes down to the context; if we can take what we've learned in the e-learning program and actually transfer it to our day job, then we've got a winner. For example, in this program on behavior in the workplace I told the story of Screaming Ruth, a manager that may have crossed the line.

Figure 8.1.   A Screen Shot From a Mocked-Up E-Learning Program

Ruth has a new member on her team who appears to be a bit inept. Her frustration with him climbs until one day she loses it in front of her other staff. Amelia, who witnesses the event, calls HR to report her. A few days later Ruth threatens the group, saying she'll find out who the traitor was. The story had lots of shades of gray to it—life is messy that way—and leaves you hanging on a cliff. What's going to happen?

I've shown this course in webinars as an example of using stories, and people always want me to show every slide of the story. Why? Because they want to know what happened. Good stories create curiosity; we want to know what's going to happen, that's why we stay up all night to finish that page-turning whodunit.

In the case of Screaming Ruth, the client was a large financial institution with employees sitting on busy trading floors, so I couldn't use audio. Instead, I relied on a text and graphics approach for the story, which we told through a series of seven "filmstrip cells." It was like creating a comic strip in a digital format. Each picture and accompanying text caption told a piece of the story. Our development team used Flash to create this program, but you could easily replicate this same approach in Articulate Presenter or Articulate Storyline or another e-learning authoring tool—even plain old PowerPoint.

When the story ends, stop and ask the participant a series of questions to help them go a little deeper, confirm their understanding, and—most importantly—forge a more memorable and lasting connection to the content. In this case, we first asked, "Did Amelia do the right thing by contacting HR?" The possible responses pick up on that gray zone and the common mistakes that people make—"Ruth was out of line, but calling HR was an overreaction" or "Ruth's behavior was inappropriate. Amelia did the right thing." This first question isn't hard to get right—in fact, it's kind of a no-brainer. Of course Ruth was out of line.

The next question takes it deeper. "Ruth's behavior was inappropriate. But why?"

Figure 8.2. A Screen Shot From a Mocked-Up E-Learning Program

The possible options to this second question get under the surface and address specific policies and workplace attitudes. Follow-up questions like this can make your scenario feel like a Socratic dialogue, peeling back the layers of the situation and exposing more gray areas. For instance, one option suggested that Ruth was wrong because she demonstrated gender discrimination against her male employee. It's a rather simplistic choice, but one that some people might infer based on how the scene unfolded. Another option suggested that it's fine to yell at people and what Ruth did wrong was threaten retaliation. This option gets to the notion that people have within the organization that it is OK to yell at people, because it's a high-stress financial environment and that type of behavior just goes with the territory.

The real challenge to writing a question like this is to make sure that each of the responses are plausible enough and target those areas where people get it wrong and misinterpret the policy. I worked closely with the client's legal team to craft options that they knew from experience were the tricky areas people fell into. It took time and they did quite a few edits to get it right.

So What's Your Story?

I may not have told a great story here, but hopefully I got you thinking about some of the ways that you can use stories in your own e-learning programs. Branching exercises, fake branching, and guided stories are more ways to weave a good story into your narrative. For more on these approaches, see chapter 4.

These are fairly simple solutions that don't mean you have to throw your budget and timelines out the window; but you can provide some simple ways to put context into your programs and provide strong cognitive hooks for your learners to latch onto. Scenarios are great for illustrating how those soft, mushy skills you're teaching look in the real world. Complex branching can be an excellent way to illustrate difficult problem solving situations—showing how someone made the decision and what the consequences were.

Regardless of which approach you end up using, remember to:

- gather your stories from real SMEs

- make the stories realistic and plausible

- explore the gray areas of a situation (not everything is black and white!)

- make questions challenging and plausible

- accurately portray the consequences

- provide valuable feedback and remediation on suboptimal choices.

When you keep these principles in mind, your scenarios will be more focused, relevant, and effective. And, if you still want to put 3D blue-haired avatars in them—be my guest. Just don't put them in instead of the good stuff.

chapter 9

Looking Good: On Visual Design

In this chapter . . .

- Why do visuals really matter?

- How can you get the visual right, even if you're not a graphic artist?

- Where can you find out more on visual design?

I know that I've raised the anti-clicky-clicky bling-bling banner and have urged you to banish extraneous bling, forego the distracting sparkle, and eliminate the animated pinwheels. Please. But I still think that looks matter. Whatever you do, don't design ugly courses.

In Susan Weinschenk's fabulous little book, *100 Things Every Designer Needs to Know about People* (2011, 177), she tells us, "people use look and feel as their first indicator of trust." Weinschenk looked at research by Elizabeth Sillence from 2004 that showed that participants decided which health websites to trust based on design factors such as "look and feel, poor navigation, color, text size, or the name of the website."

Extrapolate this to your own e-learning design and remember that first impressions matter. Your program needs to make that first cut; only then will users rate it on content and credibility. If your site looks crummy and unworthy, well, you'll never make that cut.

Consider the same phenomena in terms of pricing. Three proposals are in front of a client for the same basic services and one of them is really cheap, much cheaper than the other two. Even if they look like the same proposal, the lowest priced solution doesn't usually win. Why? Because people don't trust it. If it's that cheap, it can't be that good, right?

The same applies to visual design. Put two e-learning courses out there with the same content. One looks like a cheesy PowerPoint template, the other a thoughtfully designed piece. The nicer looking one will, quite literally, turn more heads and get better results. That trustworthiness factor creeps in and people pay more attention to the nice looking program.

Aligning to Your Brand

As a learning designer, one of your main goals it to persuade people.

Marketing departments know how to do this well. Think about some of the popular brands we recognize: Apple, Target, Starbucks, Dunkin' Donuts, Nike, the list goes on. The brand geniuses behind these companies have the power to create desire—even for something you didn't know you wanted. They're often selling an experience and a lifestyle more than the actual product.

In essence a brand is about the personality of the organization and its products or services. This personality creates thoughts, feelings, perceptions, images, experiences, beliefs, and attitudes. The sum of all the points of contact with the brand is generally known as the brand experience.

The best brands create desire and have the most passionate fans. So how can you, a learning designer, create a desire for learning? How can you create passionate fans?

In the same way brands add value to a product or service, brand-led learning can add an extra level of value to the overall learning experience. This in no way reduces the impact of good instructional design or cognitive engagement through screen-based interactions; but a learning design that's cognitively sound, yet lacks personality, is not going to fare very well at the party. There are too many other messages fighting for you learner's attention. If your program is the only one that doesn't pack a brand punch, you may as well not show up to the contest.

Brand-led e-learning incorporates the persona, value, and key messaging of the organizations. It complements solid instructional design and shows how best practice is always in sync with the core values of the organization. The way the learners are being asked to learn needs to be equally in sync with that brand and set of values.

Training and development (T&D) can have a brand within the organization. Your T&D team probably has a set of its own values and objectives—it might even have a sub-logo. But making sure your visuals are on brand is about more than slapping the logo in the top right corner. A truly branded learning experience goes beyond the visual identity guidelines to influence every aspect of the design. It's about finding the tone and messaging that effectively reflects your company's brand.

Brand-led learning not only applies to the e-learning program, but also to the delivery platform or learning management system (LMS). So often forgotten in the visual department, the LMS is the front door, so it better be on brand, too, because this is where the real first impression begins. Sadly, most LMSs have the company logo in the top left corner and lists of boring text links.

So as you think about visual design, be sure to string your brand and identity through every asset you're creating as part of a learning portal or experience.

Vision Trumps All

If you haven't read John Medina's *Brain Rules: 12 Principles for Surviving and Thriving at Work, Home, and School*, please do. It's an easy read and full of 12 juicy tidbits that make sense and apply to our work as e-learning designers. According to Medina's Rule 10, "vision trumps all other senses" (2008, 240). He goes on to tell us that "we learn and remember best through pictures, not through written or spoken words." Text and audio are way less efficient than pictures, because while words are technically pictures, our brain has to decipher them. Images take less effort to understand.

Now, this isn't about someone being a visual learner or learning styles. This is a truth for anyone that can see. More than half of our brains are devoted to the interpretation of what we see, which makes it our most dominant sense. Medina says that vision is "probably the best single tool we have for learning anything" (2008, 233).

Connie Malamed writes a wonderful blog called *The eLearning Coach*. She's also the author of *Visual Language for Designers*—a gorgeous coffeetable edition with a ton of examples that provide some practical tips to doing six key things with and through graphics:

- organizing graphics for quick perception
- directing the eyes to essential information

- using visual shorthand for efficient communication (reducing realism)

- making the abstract concrete

- clarifying complexity

- charging a graphic with energy and emotion.

As Connie Malamed explains, visuals are more than just pretty wallpaper. Well-designed screens help us understand information and make sense of complex idea.

I'm not a graphics designer, but over the years I have picked up a few tricks and tips that have worked well for me.

Make the Graphics Matter

Don't just wallpaper your screens with pretty pictures. A full screen photograph of tulips may fill the heart with awe, but it probably doesn't belong in a course on workplace safety . . . unless, of course, the tulips play a key role in a spilled vase that caused Walter, an employee at Tables to Tulips, to slip and fall.

Include graphics that are relevant and add meaning. Ruth Clark urges us to provide useful visuals because "they offer the brain an additional opportunity to build mental models" (2010, 83). Decorative visuals, like those unnecessary tulips, can actually depress learning.

Use Animation Wisely

Medina tells us that we're primed to pay attention to motion. Nancy Duarte exhorts us to design animation with purpose and meaning, otherwise we risk turning the audience's attention away from what matters. As she wrote, "animation is not last-minute icing on the cake; it's a key communication strategy" (2008, 180).

Use simple animations to demonstrate a point—even line drawings are fine. In fact, Ruth Clark tells us that simple static visuals may be more easily understood than an actual photo or more realistic 3D drawings or animation. She explains that too much visual complexity can flood us with too much information and overload memory capacity (2010, 139).

Avoiding Cheesy Stock Photos

The chess pieces to represent strategy? Yeah, we've all done that. It's cliché. And expected and boring—and sometimes all you can come up with. So at least use a cool picture of chess pieces. How about the ubiquitous diverse teamwork shot showing 10 hands on top of each other? Each hand a different color. Rah, rah, rah! Or the smiling business people staring right at the camera.

Have you ever spent time surfing a stock photo site? I admit that I have done this. On numerous occasions. Because sometimes you're searching for something reasonable and crazy stuff comes up in the results screen. Like a business man wearing yellow rubber gloves while typing on a computer with a mouse eating a piece of cheese on his shoulder. How is that relevant to anything in the real world? Or maybe I just shouldn't ask.

Avoid cheesy stock photographs and crappy clip art. Do not, I repeat, do not use those bean people drawings from the late 1990s.

So where can you get good photos and images?

- stock photo sites (you can get a subscription or buy credits)

- take your own photos

- hire a photographer to do a photo shoot

- purchase character packs or image files from sites like elearningart.com or elearningbrothers.com

- explore sites like Flickr where photographers may allow you to reuse their photos. However, be sure to understand the rules, share proper attribution, and get the photographer's permission if needed.

I won't get into copyright laws here, but just know that it's really not OK to see a cool presentation on SlideShare, download it, and then reuse all of the photos in that presentation. I have been asked by people who like my slides if they can use my photos. They're not mine. I got them through a license with a stock photography site and you cannot reuse them.

Likewise, don't just do a Google image search and think you can use any photo because it came up in your search results. That's not how it works. You may need to get permission to use those photos!

Finding the Right Partners

If you're an accidental instructional designer like me, beautiful graphic design may not ooze out of your fingertips. I have had the benefit of working in organizations where we hire specialists to do that work. We have top notch graphic designers who know user-interface design, who can find ways to visually represent ideas, and can turn blah into spectacular. If your program is going to have high visibility with high stakes, consider outsourcing your visual design. Find a professional to partner with in order to make something that your organization would be proud of, that the people in your organization would enjoy looking at, and—more importantly—that enhances the learning experience.

Going It Alone

If you don't have the resources at hand to hire graphic expertise and the burden is on your shoulders, get out there and beg, borrow, and steal.

Learn how to use the tools. PowerPoint can be a great graphics tool if you know what you're doing and aren't just importing crummy clip art and using PowerPoint templates. Popular bloggers like Tom Kuhlmann share tips and templates, and live workshops and online classes can help you make the most out of it.

Find inspiration from sites that you love and try your best to emulate them.

Get involved in online communities that share design tips and templates. Articulate has a rich and active community of people sharing their work for the betterment of the e-learning world.

Buy some templates. Google "e-learning templates" and you'll find a number of sites with template packs for sale. Purchase with a discerning eye and don't get caught up in the nine-hole golf course games or other clicky-clicky nonsense. Find templates that you can customize to make your own, but that give you a really solid starting point.

Remember, looks matter. Spend some time and energy to give your program some intentional and meaningful zing. And get help if you need it. The CBT Lady may not care about whether or not her e-learning program looks good, but you do. And so do your learners. Looks matter.

chapter 10

Mixing It Up: New Blends and Marketing Strategies

In this chapter . . .

- Why should instructional designers think less like bartenders and more like mixologists?

- What's a learning blend?

- How can you create learning campaigns that go beyond the single event?

- What about mobile?

If you're an instructional designer with a view to the big picture of performance improvement within your organization, then you know that one tool—self-paced e-learning—certainly won't be all that you need to meet the needs of the organization. Designing and developing self-paced e-learning may be where you started your career—or where you've ended up—but it's time to step back and get a bigger picture view of the different tools you can use.

As someone who cares about performance, what do you want to see people doing in your organization? Could it be some of this?

- accessing the information they need to do their jobs

- getting opportunities to practice new skills in order to integrate new knowledge into existing mental models, and ensure smooth application on the job

- having the chance to reflect on their performance and identify areas for improvement

- connecting with peers and mentors for coaching and troubleshooting

- asking questions and finding answers to problems when they're feeling stuck

- collaborating to generate new and innovative ways of working

- identifying the root causes of problems in order to find better solutions.

It's a different mindset than just providing "training," isn't it? It's about finding ways to work smarter—which is the business of, well, your business. It's not just a training team task, and if you want to make sure you stay relevant, it's important to be involved and use your expertise where it matters. This may mean stepping outside the bounds of the training and development department, putting on that consulting hat, and forging new ground.

Is It too Good to Be True?

One of the downsides to all the technology-based training that has been happening for the past 15 years (at least), is that it's really dumbed down the approach that many people take to training.

It seems a bit too good to be true to think that we can effectively train, create sustained behavior change, and facilitate deep learning in an easy-to-produce, 30-minute e-learning course. That's because it *is* too good to be true. And yet that's the mindset a lot of organizations—and those within them—seem to have: "Just create an e-learning program!"

I know, I know, this sounds like blasphemy coming from someone who has buttered her bread for 15 years by creating a lot of 30-minute e-learning courses. Today, however, we talking about flipping the classroom and putting the self-paced e-learning modules first as a way to get the information your audience needs in front of them. Then you can follow up your e-learning session with classroom and immersive sessions that let participants practice and roll play with live instructor feedback. Assign students to cohort groups for a meaningful blended experience. As they move through the program, have them reconnect with their cohorts—either live or virtually—to share experiences and provide peer-to-peer feedback. If you do it right, this blend creates a coherent learner journey, with the understanding that the learning process takes time, requires effective practice, opportunity for integration and reflection, and valuable feedback cycles from both mentors and peers.

Self-paced e-learning can be one really excellent ingredient in the mix. But instructional designers and those who care about performance would do well to expand that ingredient list. You might say it pays to become a learning mixologist.

Becoming a Mixologist

Mixologist versus bartender. There's a difference? Apparently. A bartender wipes down the bar, pours the beers on tap, opens bottles, and mixes up drinks—usually from a fairly set menu. A mixologist, on the other hand, studies the art and science of beverage making and invents new and exotic cocktails. That innovative viewpoint sets the mixologist apart from a bartender, and can set you apart from the next run-of-the-mill self-paced e-learning designer.

A learning mixologists looks for the right blends to support the needs of the organization, choosing from a wide array of ingredients and techniques: social learning, collaborative tools, performance support using mobile devices, self-paced programs, augmented reality, virtual instructor-led classes, webinars, video, live classroom sessions, immersive digital experiences, serious games, formal and informal programs, coaching, and mentoring.

Unlike a bartender who just pours the same beers for his customers year after year—or an instructional designer/trainer who delivers the same-old-same-old e-learning year after year—the learning mixologist tries out new approaches, and looks for innovative solutions to solve the problems of the business.

A learning mixologist keeps an eye on technology trends, watching for any possibilities on the horizon. The Gartner Hype Cycle for Emerging Technologies takes a look at new technologies and plots them on a curve. The beginning of the curve, the Innovation Trigger stage, is crowded with new technologies. As interest and hype for a new technology grows, it hits the Peak of Inflated Expectations. From there things quickly go downhill into the Trough of Disillusionment. Next comes the Slope of Enlightenment, and finally the Plateau of Productivity, which is essentially the mainstream. In 2013, the innovation stages of the Gartner Hype Cycle listed

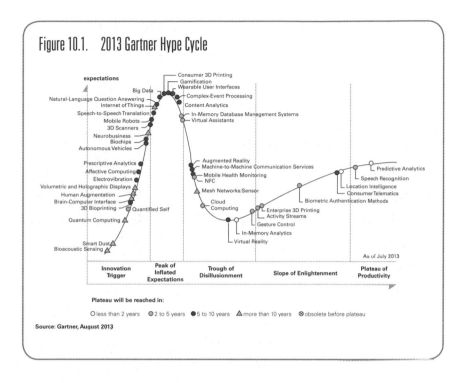

Figure 10.1. 2013 Gartner Hype Cycle

brain-computer interfaces, biochips, and 3D scanners. Currently at the peak—and expected to plateau within the next five to 10 years—are big data, consumer 3D printing, and gamification. Hitting the trough now, but hitting mainstream soon, include augmented reality, virtual reality, and enterprise 3D printing.

The 2013 Gartner Hype Cycle for Education takes a more focused look at digitalization trends on learning technologies, showing things like quantum and affective computing on the uptick; big data and MOOCs at the peak; ideas like BYOD strategies slipping into the trough; tablets climbing the slope; and e-book readers, self-publishing, and mashups hitting the plateau.

How will these technologies and trends affect learning and training in your lifetime and in your organizations? I can't say for sure, except that they will. A learning mixologist knows this and isn't afraid to try on Google Glass to see what all the fuss is about and where the promise might lie for organizations. A learning mixologist prepares for this inevitable future and looks for ways to stay professionally relevant to better serve the needs of the employees of the future.

What About Social Learning?

Let's talk about hype. A long, long time ago "social learning" was all the rage. Right? That's been the buzz of the last few years. But frankly, all this social learning and social business talk freaks a lot of business leaders out. That's crazy. Maybe they're picturing a cocktail party with lampshades on people's heads? They need to relax. We're all social, man.

Social learning has been around since the dawn of time. It's how cavemen learned to make fire. A spark ignited a dead tree. The cavemen shared the fire with each other. They showed each other how to tend the fire and how to make more. Then they told stories about making fire, while sitting around the campfire. (Or at least, that's what one would expect.)

Enter Continuous, Collaborative Learning

And so, as with most learning trends, the language changes and the concept expands. Today we hear more talk more about creating a collaborative workplace than a social one. It doesn't sound like quite the cocktail party does it? Sounds more like grown-up people doing good work together.

The other term we hear attached to collaborative learning is "continuous." Because learning never ends. We're lifelong learners and there is always more to learn, something to improve, and something new to master.

Which brings me to . . . oh, I forget. Oh yeah.

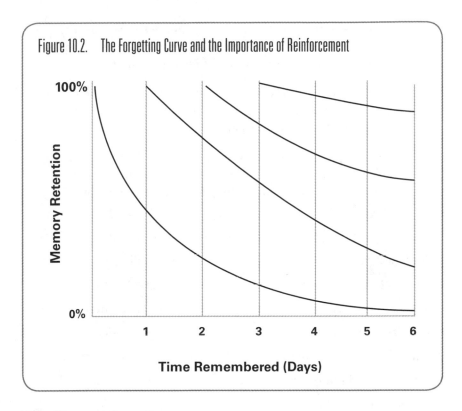

Figure 10.2.   The Forgetting Curve and the Importance of Reinforcement

The Forgetting Curve

The Forgetting Curve reminds us that people really do forget.

The Ebbinghaus Forgetting Curve plots how information is lost when there is no effort to review or retain the material. The curve represents the average learner and can be influenced by a number of things. I first learned about the Forgetting Curve from Will Thalheimer, who explains there are many variables that affect how much we will forget and by when, including how memorable and meaningful the content presentation was (stories pack more punch!), how relevant the material is, and the person's prior knowledge (Thalheimer, 2010).

The bottom line: humans forget stuff. According to Thalheimer, your best bet as a learning professional who wants to help people remember better, is to use three proven methods:

- Align the learning and performance **contexts**: Use realistic, contextual practice exercises and scenario-based questions to mimic the real world and ensure better transfer on-the-job.

- Provide **retrieval practice**: Provide practice opportunities that mimic the real world situation in which the learner will have to retrieve and use this information.

- Provide **spaced repetitions**: Instead of dumping all the content and practice opportunities into one single learning event, space them out over time to help forge stronger memories and better encoding.

If we space things out, people are more likely to remember. So, yes, let's make it continuous! Let's never stop, and keep finding opportunities to help people discover, connect, process, experience, and learn.

At a recent ASTD conference, Arthur Kohn, a neuropsychologist specializing in learning and memory, gave the presentation, "Brain and Memory: Seven Tips That Improve E-Learning." He championed the spacing effective and shared his recommendations for creating a spaced learning sequence.

Following the initial session, Kohn suggests reconnecting with the learners three times. Two days after the session, he says to quiz them on a piece of critical information. For example, "According to the instructor, what was the most important first step?" This question focuses on fact-based recall. Two weeks later, ask a question to elicit elaborative recall: "Hey, according to that lecture on XXX how can you imagine using that information in our organization?" He suggests having the student provide a written response, but you could bake this strategy into your learning program in a lot of different ways, including social media tools (I'm thinking Facebook groups or a forum on your internal platform). After two months, Kohn says to reconnect with them yet again. This time ask, "Can you give us examples of how you've used this in your organization?" This point really helps the learners see how they've transferred this information or skill back to the workplace and into their performance.

Kohn's bottom line? No one learns from a single pass. We do better by reconnecting, refreshing, and spacing out the content. Because people forget so easily, we need to remember this as we design learning experiences and factor the forgetting into the trail of resources, events, and materials that we scatter about in the hopes that people will learn from them.

Today, more and more technology-based tools offer the promise of helping out with training reinforcement and spaced learning. Even a smart LMS can be used to serve up content over time to individuals through a spaced schedule and with greater personalization based on learning needs.

Continuous Learning, Meet the Learning Campaign

I first heard the term "learning campaign" while interviewing Brent Schlenker in 2009 for the Kineo website. When I was starting my journey from becoming an accidental instructional designer to an intentional one, Brent was one of the first bloggers I found who wrote about learning and when I commented on his blog—and he actually replied back—it was very exciting. In our interview, Brent talked about the need to move away from self-paced learning events and to start thinking in terms of learning campaigns.

We've all heard of ad campaigns. Advertisers are relentless. They know how to get into our brains, incite our desire and curiosity, and get us to buy. Bottom line, marketers know how to change behavior better than almost anyone. Isn't that what we're all trying to do? The idea of a learning campaign—lots of touch points spread out over time—makes a lot of sense. In fact, the real secret to behavior change may be a sustained campaign—that is, multiple content touch points over a sustained period of time that keep reinforcing key messages, in order to create motivation and desire to act, and the tools and skills to put that action into place.

Think about the public service announcements (PSA). During World War II, posters, short films, and radio spots created awareness around health and safety issues in the United States and the United Kingdom. The "Keep Calm and Carry On" poster was originally created in 1939 England, but it has taken on new meaning in the 21st century. A touch of propaganda, perhaps, but a focus on public interest at the time. In the United States, the Ad Council (started in 1941 as the War Advertising Council), led the famous "Loose Lips Sink Ships" campaign, followed by Smokey the Bear. And who could forget the classic 1980s TV-spots from the Partnership for a Drug Free America, "This is your brain on drugs," showing a fried egg sizzling in a hot pan. PSA campaigns are effective at changing behaviors with long lasting cultural stickiness.

What do PSAs do really well? High-impact headlines and slogans, strong visuals, powerful messages that hit at a deep emotional core, and sustained messaging in a variety of formats. No "one hit wonders"; instead you see variations of the messaging over a long period of time—something to consider as you embark on creating a learning campaign.

Marketing professionals are in the persuasion business. They work to stimulate demand. Who are you trying to reach? With what message? Where do those people hang out? How do we use those channels? How are we going to get action? What is the campaign theme? How will we know if it's working? They ask these questions. And, as a learning professional, so should you.

If you really want to change behavior, don't start from the position of event-driven, adult-to-child enforcement—as is so often the way of the self-paced e-learning program. It's like the stern mother telling her children to wipe their mouths and clean up their rooms, or else. Whereas this may be a fine way to raise polite and tidy children, it's no way for adults within organizations to treat the other adults in that same organization. It creates resentment, annoyance, and noncompliance. Most of us don't like being treated like children now that we're grown.

At Kineo, we've been taking a closer look at the area of content marketing as we think about creating learning campaigns that attract people, engage them, and drive behavior. Content marketing is more than just advertising a product. Content marketers create relevant and valuable content. For instance, a diaper company may have a blog or publication with useful tips for new parents—above and beyond the simple cleaning of bottoms. With this content, the diaper company wants to create consumers loyal to their brand, customers who look to the brand for expertise and wisdom because they trust it. Of course, in the end, the diaper company wants to sell more diapers. Social tools like Facebook pages and Twitter accounts make this content marketing an even more powerful tool, because people share and redistribute brand-generated information—at no additional cost to the company.

In simple terms, marketing aims to:

- Attract and convert prospects into advocates and believers, even raving fans.

- Use a range of channels and techniques that are specifically designed to reach the target audience(s).

- Create a sustained campaign that evolves and responds based on early feedback, and brings about measurable results.

Think about it. A learning campaign is something you can do. You're a learning mixologist. You're ready to innovate and try something that really works. Why not?

A learning campaign makes an ongoing effort to impact behavior. It's a great approach for a compliance program. Use it for those nitpicky behavior change messages that people need to delete their emails as they go along and share files using share sites instead of emails to keep digital foot-prints down and ensure the final record is where it needs to be—"one copy, one place!" Compliance training is so often treated as a one-off event, but we'd be better off getting people to think about it every day until it comes to them as naturally as locking their own front door.

So a part of this is to space it out, right? Remember that forgetting curve? You might find that the best way to meet a learning objective is by producing a string or blend of experiences that extend across different deliv-ery mediums and over a spaced calendar. In this way, you create a learning campaign rather than a single, static event. The output may include self-paced e-learning courses, classroom based activities, online webinars, post-ers in the cafeteria, YouTube style videos, email reminders, checklists, and performance support tools. This isn't about marketing the learning itself, but using marketing tools to spread the learning content. See the difference?

So let's change the conversation and find ways to make this happen in our organizations.

how could we do this?

Case Study

Not Your Average Compliance Program—The Change Campaign

A global entertainment company had, what some could interpret as, dry content. They had policies and steps that people needed to follow, or else big trouble could happen to the company, their actors, and their em-ployees. They needed to:

- raise awareness about threats to privacy and information security

- get people to take compliance-related policies seriously

- empower people to take action.

Because they're an entertainment company it wasn't in their culture to do boring. They wanted to engage attention and deliver results. So, they embarked on a change campaign that spanned a number of years (and is still ongoing). They didn't even go all Hollywood on the budget. Here's what they pulled together over time:

- Short but creative video stories featuring two mumbling but memorable characters. Throughout the video, key tips with catchy titles are flashed onscreen.

- Posters and flyers, which they distributed throughout their campuses, featuring the two characters. This built brand equity for the campaign and also reinforced those catchy tip titles.

- Catchy jingles!

- Chocolates with QR codes on the packaging that brought people to a video trailer promoting the e-learning initiative.

- Themed cafeteria menus that tied into the security messages.

- Tip sheets and decoder wheels to reinforce key skills and provide quick reference aids for use on the job.

- Focused, self-paced e-learning tutorials and how-tos, underscoring key policy and regulation campaign messages to teach the skills and provide practice, once again featuring those beloved characters.

The organization asked people to change, they kept the messages coming, and they rewarded participation.

The results? Impressive. Not only was the employee feedback on the program really great, but, more importantly the numbers showed success: more employees reached out for help; the chief privacy officer got more requests for guidance on training, tools, and rules; and project teams started reaching out to legal and information security for help on their initiatives earlier than ever before.

Change Is Coming

In his keynote speech at the ASTD's 2013 International Conference, John Seely Brown, a researcher who writes about education and digital culture, talked about how the world has changed. And it has, right? A hundred years ago we educated people and trained them for factory jobs. There were standards and ways of doing things.

Today, many of us are part of an increasingly connected and global, knowledge-based economy where the challenges are more complex. Even in traditional industries like manufacturing, rapid changes in technology require more open and innovative ways of working, and of thinking, while on the job. With technologies changing so fast, Brown suggests that the half-life of any skill is shrinking to less than five years, which means that a skill today will be redefined in 10 years. That's hard to keep up.

When you think about how quickly things are changing today, we have to learn a lot of information really quickly. The challenge is that we haven't had the time to figure out the explicit component of that knowledge—nor will we have the time as things just continue to change. A lot of the knowledge is still tacit and in our heads. Tacit knowledge can't be delivered by traditional training techniques.

We don't have time to do training the way we've been doing it! And so we've seen people finding new ways to connect with each other and get the information they need. Twitter and internal networks spring up—the water coolers of the digital world—to ask colleagues questions, find answers, and go outside the walls of your office and company. Work *is* social.

Brown explains that we've moved from the old order of corporate training, where materials were packaged in big binders (think "stocks") to a new world that no longer receives well-structured assets (think "flow"). Knowledge is fluid and evolving and to participate in the flow, well, we need to go with it. We need to create knowledge and participate in that creation. In this new era, the teacher no longer transfers knowledge, he becomes a coach or mentor.

So let's go with the flow. As Harold Jarche says, "Work is learning and learning is work" (2012). Because businesses need to adapt to this changing world, learning as we go along how we work.

Jane Hart and Jay Cross created a schematic for the Five Stages of Workplace Learning, which lays out the evolution of the modern workplace:

stage 1: classroom training

stage 2: e-learning

stage 3: blended learning

stage 4: social learning

stage 5: collaborative learning/working.

As they move from stage 1 to stage 5, organizations go from a much more controlled and formal learning environment, to one that is more autonomous, collaborative, and informal. The most evolved organizations have gone beyond social to collaborative (Cross and Hart, 2011).

Jane Hart's Learning in the Workplace Survey 2013 reinforced this message, showing that the methods organizations use for communication, learning, and engagement need to change. Survey respondents gave company training/e-learning the lowest ratings among ways to learn at work, while giving a thumbs up to other (self-organized and self-managed) ways of learning at work—with team collaboration being the highest rated. People are practically begging us to move away from self-contained training events and more toward embedded, less formal activities, including active searching, conversations with colleagues, and continuous communication channels and networking.

There are a lot of things pointing toward this need to change things up, aren't there? So how do you foster collaboration in your organization?

Well, it helps if you start with a culture that already values collaboration. If you've got a tightly siloed workplace, where no one likes to share ideas, then putting collaborative tools in place to foster conversation and build connections likely won't work. But if people are primed for collaboration, then you may be ready to use collaborative workplace tools and social business platforms like Jive or Podio.

How Can Training and Development Help?

Talking about the full-scale implementation of a collaborative business tool is beyond the scope of this book (and me), but from a learning department standpoint, know that this can be your territory. Training and development people—and those who care about performance—can help, but how?

Here are a few ways that the training department can get involved as your organization starts thinking more collaboratively:

- community management
- mentorship and reverse mentorship programs
- working with IT to get the right tools in place
- content curation (filtering the most relevant and useful content to the top of the pile so it's more easily discovered and shared).

New 21st-century roles, like community managers and online discussion moderators, situate us to tie conversations together and help people find one another while we look for stories worth retelling and expertise worth capturing.

The prolific Jane Bozarth, whose newest book is called *Show Your Work*, urges individuals and organizations to narrate our work as we go along, making the tacit explicit (2013). She says we can do this through blogs, narrated PowerPoint decks or screen casts, and YouTube-style videos (where you talk about why you're doing something the way that you're doing it, not just what you're doing—be explicit about the thought process behind the decisions you make). By showing our work, and encouraging our peers and employees to do the same, we create a culture that goes with the flow and helps people reflect more on their own experiences. Reflection ensures better integration knowledge transfer to our jobs and means that we share that tacit knowledge with others.

So What About Mobile?

In 2013, we still see most of our clients hovering around the edge of smartphones as vehicles for training and performance improvement materials. Everyone still wants desktop delivery, whereas more and more clients are asking for tablet versions. But frankly, people are still treading cautiously around what to put on a phone and how. As more and more organizations move to a bring-your-own-device model, however, this reluctance is changing. The good news is that people increasingly realize that you can't just put a course on a phone.

Clark Quinn and Chad Udell both have great books on mobile design and best use cases of mobile learning and content. Think about just-in-time performance support or quick refresher nuggets, keeping the mobile use case in mind. If you're not sure what I mean, consider how you use your own phone. Do you spend 30 minutes at a time looking at one thing on your phone? Or would you rather sit down with a tablet or laptop for those longer experiences? Are you tapping your phone for a quick reference or how-to? Watching a three-minute video? Maybe, just maybe, you're reading a book on your Kindle app while you're stuck in the doctor's office waiting room and you don't have your tablet. Or, you find yourself watching a feature length movie on your phone during that red-eye flight from San Francisco to Boston. We use our devices a little differently depending on context.

Keep track of your own usage and ask your employees what they're doing—and what they would like to have access to—on their mobile devices.

Organizations want to future-proof their content—believing that if they go in the direction of HTML5 instead of Flash they will save themselves some pain and suffering down the line. At Kineo, we've been exploring responsive web design, in the form of an open-source authoring tool called Adapt. Responsive design means that the application scales and changes—it responds—depending on the size of the screen on which you're viewing it. You can tag content elements for viewing only on desktop, or remove some elements from the phone display depending on how you think people will be using and accessing the content. It's a new way of thinking about e-learning content—think web pages with learning content, rather than slide-based learning programs. The cool thing about Adapt and responsive web design approaches is that they transcend the device—it's not just about mobile anymore. And if you think about the ways you access content in your real life these days you know this makes sense. Right now I am working on my laptop with my smartphone at my side and my tablet not far away—I want to be able to get to the information I need regardless of the device I'm using. Tools like Adapt enable you to create one program that can easily be delivered across devices, giving you greater flexibility in how you reach people and connect them with content that matters.

Think Learning Portals

Traditional learning management systems provide a pretty unblended way of looking at content: lists of courses you can take and that's about it. You may want to open things up by moving beyond an LMS to a more portal-based approach.

What's a learning portal? Think entry point to content; conversation and shared resources about a particular topic. You could have a portal within your organization that focuses on information security. It could house courses, PDFs, discussion groups, collaborative tools, videos links to external websites, and RSS feeds pulling in the latest information security news from the Internet. You can still get the tracking and back end data that you want, but more importantly you're putting curated information that people can use in one place, while features that allow learners to tailor their content create a truly personalized space for learning and content acquisition. This is where people can solve the problems they need to solve. At Kineo, we're fans of open source and use Totara—an open source distribution of Moodle for the corporate sector—to create learning portals for organizations. It's really about creating a place that people want to go because there's so much rich content in one centralized hub. And we'll continue to see traditional LMS suppliers adding these feature sets to their systems to create more flexible portal-like solutions.

So, 2013 presents a lot of new technology options. It's bit confusing and overwhelming if you're used to PowerPoint-style content dumps. But, we've got a lot more options as learning designers, which can only mean good things—*if* we do it right and don't just create more content dreck.

Case Study

Mixing It Up With New Blends At Coats

Coats is the world's leading industrial thread and consumer textile crafts business, with locations in more than 70 countries, and over 20,000 people across six continents. As the organization set new strategic goals and increased its focus on product innovation, it knew it needed to build its leadership capabilities from within.

So, how does a large global organization implement a global leadership program for frontline and middle managers, many of whom have never had formal leadership training?

The solution involves the smart use of technology, while also building in appropriate face-to-face time, mentoring, and support for leaders. Some people call that "blended learning," but it's really just common sense and making the right use of the right modalities available to an organization and that meet the needs of the employees.

Coats created a two-year blended leadership development program, which opens with a two-day face-to-face workshop with managers gathering together in cohorts of 20 from all over the world to learn the basics of Coats's leadership framework. Many of these managers have had little or no formal leadership training, so there is a lot of ground to cover. Over the next 16 months, participants are introduced to eight core leadership competencies. Each competency is given a two-month window, during which individuals complete about 45 minutes of self-paced e-learning modules, broken into a series of short modules. The e-learning modules provide an introduction to key concepts, within the context of the Coats's environment. Four characters, each based on different Coats personas, are the key players in the e-learning program, providing fertile ground for realistic examples and scenarios that people can apply to their situation at Coats.

Activities within each module provide the learners with the opportunity to extend their learning outside of the program and take it into the real world. For instance, in a module on decision making, the learners are asked to print out a copy of the decision-making toolkit from the resources tab, identify a decision that they need to make, and then use the toolkit to work through each step. These exercises make the content less abstract and more about real-life application.

Once the participant completes the e-learning program on a particular competency, the learning management system sets up a triggered event: the employee has to sit down for a coaching session with his or her own manager. Conversation guides and tools are provided to help the manager coach and support the employee going through the program. Once the manager signs off on that employee's progress, he or she can then move along to the next stage in the curriculum.

Meanwhile, all the course participants are assigned cohort groups within the LMS, along with a "buddy." Through forum discussions in the LMS, peer-to-peer sharing sessions, and regular real-word check-ins, participants stay connected and share their experiences with each other.

As the months go on, webinars are made available to the course delegates on topics ranging from performance management to providing better feedback. Halfway through the curriculum, a review and consolidation webinar is convened. These instructor-led virtual classrooms provide insight into tools and methods, give the learner a chance to check in with an instructor, and keep the leadership concepts alive and omnipresent. Once the e-learning portion of the program is completed, participants reconvene in their original group for a one-day consolidation workshop.

Mix It Up

Some might say it's a brave new world out there. There's a shiny object mentality that many people in business get distracted by—remember the peak of the Garnter Hype Cycle? Unless you're one of the brave souls and early adopters out there exploring how these tools and technologies can be used, you've probably got to keep the hype on your peripheral vision and keep getting your day job done. And yet it's important to stay on top of the trends and the new technologies, as some of them will eventually make it to the mainstream and provide new opportunities for improving performance within your organizations.

As a learning mixologist, you can step outside the self-paced e-learning solution and find other tools and solutions to pull into the mix, innovating to get the blend right.

chapter 11

Secret Handshakes

In this chapter . . .

- Theory? You're going to make us talk about theory? But I just want to DO stuff! I know, I know. But it's not so bad.

The Secret Handshakes of Instructional Design

The first e-learning conference I ever went to was in 2007. I was awestruck and felt like I was walking among giants. Or at least people way smarter than me.

I was in a session (or maybe it was a roundtable lunch) sitting across from someone who was having a moment of connection with the speaker. "Oh, Malcom Knowles. Andragogy. Great book," said the guy as they both nodded their heads and smiled knowing smiles. "It's in the bookstore."

They clearly knew some inner secret.

And me? I smiled, too, but inside I wondered, "Andragogy? What the heck is that?" So I immediately wandered off to the bookstore and bought the book, because clearly this was something I needed to know.

What I had just witnessed, what I had just become a part, of was what Ellen Wagner (2011) calls "the secret handshakes of instructional design." Those "in the know" drop names and theories and then wait for that moment of recognition from the person with whom they're conversing. "Aah, yes, she's heard of Vgotsky. She must know her instructional design stuff." Or, "Well, if we follow Bloom's Taxonomy here then we'll be fine." The names and theories are dropped, and then everyone moves on to actually get their work done.

I have had this experience with clients, fellow designers, and human resources types. Name and theory dropping happens. And even if you're an accidental designer, it pays to get a shot or two of theory.

A Little Shot of Theory

"It's just a little pinch. It'll hardly hurt and then it will be over." Tell that to a four-year-old, sitting in the doctor's office waiting for a shot.

But it turns out to be true. You take a deep breath, feel the pinch, and then move on. OK—maybe you cried a lot and maybe your arm feels bruised. But if you're good, you might get a lollipop from your mom.

I'm not talking about administering vaccinations to all you learning designers out there—although it would be nice if someone could develop a vaccine for bad e-learning! I'm suggesting that all of us take some time to learn about learning theory and instructional design theory. Sounds painful, but really, it's just a pinch.

So how do we get by? We learn the trade on the job, watch what others are doing that works, and follow our gut. Sometimes that intuition is right on; sometimes it misses the mark completely.

Practice With Intention

If you're practicing the ID craft with intention, you're probably not missing the mark quite as often as most accidental instructional designers. To practice with intention, you know what instructional strategies to use, and why, to help maximize the learning. This means you probably know a bit about learning theory and instructional design theory.

Now, some of you that went to school in instructional design or education might say, "of course you need to know theory." And I won't argue with you. Instead, let's look at a few reasons to give yourself a shot of theory.

So You Can Talk the Talk

Your clients will drop these names and expect you to understand. If you don't they may lose faith in you before you can even prove your stuff. Also, you sound really smart when you use the word "cognitive" in a sentence. Trust me.

Credibility

Another plus for those who have taken the self-education route—you sound like more of an expert.

When you actually know this stuff, well, then you can actually talk like you know this stuff. I'm not suggesting you enter client meetings rattling off names like Gagné and Reigeluth and Keller for no reason. You risk sounding like a pompous know-it-all smarty pants. I'm saying that maybe you should be a smarty pants and learn more about the research and theory behind the practice. When you talk like you know what you're talking about, you have more credibility. Of course, you also need to follow through and deliver, but sounding like you really know what you're talking about gives you a great start.

So You Can Design Better Learning Experiences

Yeah, it really does help you if you have an inkling of how adults learn and know solid strategies for how to help facilitate that process.

When you know a bit of theory, you can look at your content and apply the best strategy. You can start blending a bit of the science of ID with the art that you already practice. You can effectively explain to a client why it's really not a good idea to start a program off with the detailed flow chart, or why locking out navigation leads to learner frustration. When you educate yourself, you can educate your clients and create better learning experiences for everyone!

Here's a starting list for you of names, topics, and theories that you may want to explore as you continue on your journey from accident to intention.

Main theories of learning:

- Behaviorism: behavior can be changed through conditioning and external rewards and penalties. (Think Pavlov's dog.)

- Cognitivism: learning theories based on what goes on inside your brain.

- Constructivism: learning happens as individuals construct meaning from their own experiences and environment. We "construct" our own meaning based on our own unique viewpoints.

- Connectivism: in the digital age, learning happens by connecting through your network to access the information you need when you need it.

Once you've got your head wrapped around the big schools of thought, dive down more deeply into these theorists and theories:

- Andragogy (Knowles)

- Bloom's Taxonomy (Bloom)

- Scaffolding (Bruner)

- Zone of Proximal Development (Vygotsky)

- Nine Events of Learning/Conditions of Learning (Gagne)

- Social Learning Theory (Bandura)

- Cognitive Load Theory (Sweller)

- ARCS Model of Motivational Design (Keller)

- Maslow's Hierarchy of Needs (Maslow)

- Elaboration Theory (Reigeluth)

- Experiential Learning (Kolb)

You could make a life-long study of these theories and other new models that are probably being developed as we speak. Have an open mind, dig in with gusto, and don't be afraid to ask questions out loud. Remember, you're on a path to intentional designer and learning the secret handshakes will help you earn your membership to the club.

part III

chapter 12

Taking It Forward

In this chapter . . .

- Will you embrace this world?
- What will you do next?

So here we are. Little yellow ducks dropped into a sea, swimming in the opposite direction from the masses. We got here by accident, but it turns out we like it here. We like e-learning, we like instructional design, and we like helping people perform better. We think we make a difference and we mean to be the best ducks we can be—moving from accident to intention. We have purpose and we have found our people: each other.

Let this book be a gateway—a first step on your journey from an accidental instructional designer to an intentional one. So what can you do next?

Find Your Peers and Share Your Work

Read blogs on e-learning and instructional design. While you're at it, start your own blog to document and share what you're learning. My blog got me connected to a whole world of e-learning professionals who had already made that commitment and were willing to share their knowledge.

Find your peers. They are out there—on social networks like Twitter, at conferences, in online communities like Articulate's E-Learning Heroes. They share their work, write books, celebrate their successes, and document their failures. You can learn from them; they can learn from you. You don't have to go this alone, because you aren't. And you don't need to reinvent wheels that have already been invented.

For a starting point, check out Jane Hart's list of workplace learning professionals who blog and/or tweet at http://c4lpt.co.uk/social-learning-handbook/workplace-learning-professionals-who-blog-andor-tweet/.

Connect in Person

Go to e-learning conferences (the eLearning Guild's DevLearn and ASTD's TechKnowledge are two great ones). It really does make a difference to connect face-to-face with other people who are in the trenches doing what you're doing.

Read, Read, Read

Read books on e-learning and general design. Throughout this book, I've shared a lot of book titles that have helped me on my journey and I'm always adding new things to my wish list. You'll find a list of some of my favorite resources at the end of this book. Look for resources generated by those within the e-learning community, but also explore topics that go beyond—design, marketing, graphics, business. Inspiration and insight lie around almost every corner if you're willing to look for it. If you're passionate about this work, you really shouldn't mind staying up late on a work night to read about better design. Do it because you love to.

Find Your Go-To Resource

Check out the Kineo website. Yeah, I work for Kineo, I know. But many years ago, I was just a fan and read all of the rapid guides and top tips. It opened my eyes to better e-learning practice and, well, here I am.

But don't just copy me. Find your own resources or list of places you can go to for inspiration, encouragement, and knowledge.

Think Like a Mixologist

Be more of a mixologist than a bartender. Don't just use the same old recipe day after day, but think like an innovative cook, willing to try out new blends and sauces to see what happens. Ask people to taste them and see what they like, and—more importantly—find out what makes a difference to the business in terms of measurable results and outcomes.

Never Stop

Although I have been an instructional designer of technology-based learning for more than 15 years, I will never know it all. I can't stay on top of all the ongoing advancements in technology that make up this ever-changing field. And as an inherently insecure human being, I will never have complete confidence in my skills and knowledge. Perhaps my entry into this field by accident adds to that insecurity. As an accidental instructional designer, I worry that I'll be called out as an impostor or fraud. But this self-doubting tendency keeps me humble. The right touch of humility keeps you open, with a willingness to learn and improve. When you keep a beginners mindset, you lead your actions with a desire for greater intention.

I will never stop being an accident. And yet I can speak with the expertise of years of experience and with an open mind to learning and exploring new things. I hope you will join me on this journey and take part in the collective discovery. While my wish for you is that you don't become the CBT Lady, my even greater wish is that you, too, never stop being a happy accident.

My Favorite Resources

Blogs, Books, and Websites

Michael Allen, *Michael Allen's Guide to E-Learning: Building Interactive, Fun, and Effective Learning Programs for Any Company* (Hoboken, NJ: John Wiley and Sons, 2003).

Peter Block, *Flawless Consulting: A Guide to Getting Your Expertise Used* (New York: John Wiley and Sons, 2011).

Tim Brown, *Change by Design: How Design Thinking Transforms Organizations and Inspires Innovation* (New York: HarperCollins, 2009).

Jane Bozarth, *Better than Bullet Points: Creating Engaging e-Learning with PowerPoint* (San Francisco: Pfeiffer, 2008).

Jill Butler, Kritina Holden, and William Lidwell, *Universal Principles of Design* (Beverly, MA: Rockport Publishers, 2011).

Ruth Clark and Richard Mayer, *E-Learning and the Science of Instruction: Proven Guidelines for Consumers and Designers of Multimedia Learning* (San Francisco: Pfeiffer, 2007).

John Cross, Jay Cross, and Lance Dublin, *Implementing E-Learning* (Alexandria, VA: ASTD Press, 2002).

Julie Dirksen, *Design for How People Learn* (Berkeley, CA: New Riders, 2012).

Nancy Duarte, *Resonate: Present Visual Stories That Transform Audiences* (New York: John Wiley and Sons, 2010).

Nancy Duarte, *slide:ology: The Art and Science of Creating Great Presentations* (Sebastopol, CA: O'Reilly Media, 2008).

Kineo, Elearning Top Tips, www.kineo.com/us/resources/top-tips.

Natalie Goldberg, *Writing Down the Bones: Freeing the Writer Within* (Boston, MA: Shambhala Publications, 2005).

Jane Hart, Centre for Learning and Performance Technologies, http://c4lpt.co.uk.

Chip Heath and Dan Heath, *Made to Stick: Why Some Ideas Survive and Others Die* (New York: Random House, 2008).

Karl Kapp, *Kapp Notes* (blog), http://karlkapp.com/kapp-notes.

Tom Kuhlmann, *The Rapid e-Learning Blog*, www.articulate.com/rapid-elearning.

Learning Solutions Magazine, http://www.learningsolutionsmag.com.

Connie Malamed, *The eLearning Coach* (blog), http://theeelearningcoach.com.

Connie Malamed, *Visual Language for Designers: Principles for Creating Graphics That People Understand* (Beverly, MA: Rockport Publishers, 2011).

Matthew May, *In Pursuit of Elegance: Why the Best Ideas Have Something Missing* (New York: Broadway Books, 2010).

John Media, *Brain Rules: 12 Principles for Surviving and Thriving at Work, Home, and School* (Seattle, WA: Pear Press, 2008).

Cathy Moore, *Cathy Moore: Let's Save the World From Boring Training!* (blog), http://blog.cathy-moore.com.

Don Norman, *The Design of Everyday Things* (New York: Basic Books, 2013).

Daniel Pink, *To Sell is Human: The Surprising Truth About Moving Others* (Riverhead Trade, 2013).

Garr Reynolds, *Presentation Zen: Simple Ideas on Presentation Design and Delivery* (Berkeley, CA: New Riders, 2012).

Trina Rimmer, "Visual Design Makeover Manual," Rimmer Creative Group, January 16, 2013, http://trinarimmer.com/2013/01/16/makeover-manual.

Will Thalheimer, *Will at Work Learning* (blog), www.willatworklearning.com.

Susan Weinschenk, *100 Things Every Designer Needs to Know About People* (Berkeley, CA: New Riders, 2011).

Robin Williams, *The Non-Designer's Design Book* (Berkeley, CA: Peachpit Press, 2008).

Conferences:

ASTD TechKnowledge, www.tkconference.org.

eLearning Guild conferences, especially DevLearn and Learning Solutions, www.elearningguild.com.

Training Magazine's Annual Conference, www.trainingconference.com.

Selected Bibliography

Abel, S. (2013). "Content Strategists Must Become Engineers of Content-Driven Customer Experiences." *The Content Wrangler* (blog), July 29, http://thecontentwrangler.com/2013/07/29/content-strategists-must-become-engineers-of-content-driven-customer-experiences.

Allen, M. (2003). *Michael Allen's Guide to E-Learning: Building Interactive, Fun, and Effective Learning Programs for Any Company.* Hoboken, NJ: John Wiley and Sons.

ASTD. (2013). "$164.2 Billion Spent on Training and Development by U.S. Companies." *ASTD Blog*, December 12, www.astd.org/Publications/Blogs/ASTD-Blog/2013/12/ASTD-Releases-2013-State-of-the-Industry-Report.

Atleson, J. (2009). "The Various Roles of Instructional Design (Part I)." *Jonathan's ID* (blog), June 5, http://jonathansid.blogspot.com/2009/06/various-roles-of-instructional-design.html.

Baumeister, R., E. Bratslavsky, C. Finkenauer, and K. Vohs. (2001). "Bad is Stronger Than Good." *Review of General Psychology* 5(4): 323-370.

Bean, C. (2013a). "Brain and Memory with Arthur Kohn #ASTD2013." *Cammy Bean's Learning Visions* (blog), January 31, http://cammybean.kineo.com/2013/01/brain-and-memory-with-arthur-kohn.html.

Bean, C. (2013b). "John Seeley Brown Keynote at #ASTD2013." *Cammy Bean's Learning Visions* (blog), May 21, http://cammybean.kineo.com/2013/05/john-seeley-brown-keynote-at-astd2013.html.

Bean, C. (2012). "Making More Interactive E-Learning." Kineo Top Tips, September 2, www.kineo.com/resources/top-tips/learning-strategy-and-design/making-more-interactive-e-learning.

Bean, C. (2011). "Ethan Edwards: 5 Most Important Analysis Questions You'll Ever Ask #devlearn." *Cammy Bean's Learning Visions* (blog), November 3, http://cammybean.kineo.com/2011/11/ethan-edwards-5-most-important-analysis.html.

Bean, C. (2010a). "And a Clicky-Clicky Bling-Bling to You!" *Cammy Bean's Learning Visions* (blog), December 8, http://cammybean.kineo.com/2010/12 /and-clicky-clicky-bling-bling-to-you.html.

Bean, C. (2010b). "Learning From the Ad Men." Kineo Top Tips, July 2, www.kineo .com/us/resources/top-tips/learning-strategy-and-design/learning-from-the -ad-men.

Bean, C. (2010c). "Three Ways to Use Scenarios." Kineo Top Tips, June 14, www .kineo.com/resources/top-tips/learning-strategy-and-design/three-ways-to -use-scenarios.

Bean, C. (2010d). "Why a Shot of Theory is Good for You." Kineo Top Tips, February 14, www.kineo.com/resources/top-tips/learning-strategy-and-design /a-shot-of-theory-kellers-arcs-model.

Bean, C. (2009a). "A Shot of Theory - Keller's ARCS Model." Kineo Top Tips, December 17, www.kineo.com/us/resources/top-tips/learning-strategy-and -design/why-a-shot-of-theory-is-good-for-you.

Bean, C. (2009b). "Our Objection to Learning Objectives." Kineo Top Tips, July 18, www.kineo.com/resources/top-tips/learning-strategy-and-design /our-objection-to-learning-objectives.

Bozarth, J. (2013). "Show Your Work." ASTD webcast. June 11, www.astd.org /Digital-Resources/Webcasts/TD/2013/06/Show-Your-Work.

Brower, B. (2011). "Eyes Take Gossip to Heart." *Science News*, May 19, www .sciencenews.org/article/eyes-take-gossip-heart.

Brown, J.S. "A New Culture of Learning for a World of Constant Change: Entrepreneurial Learners." American Society for Training & Development 2013 International Conference Dallas, Texas, May 21, 2013.

Clark, R. (2010). *Evidence-Based Training Methods: A Guide for Training Methods*. Alexandria, VA: ASTD Press.

Clark, R., and R. Mayer. (2007). *E-learning and the Science of Instruction: Proven Guidelines for Consumers and Designers of Multimedia Learning*. San Francisco: Pfeiffer.

Clark, R., and R. Mayer. (2003). *E-learning and the Science of Instruction: Proven Guidelines for Consumers and Designers of Multimedia Learning*. San Francisco: Jossey-Bass.

Cross, J., and J. Hart. (2011). "5 Stages of Workplace Learning Revisited." *Learning in the Workplace* (blog), Centre for Learning and Performance Technologies, December 6, www.c4lpt.co.uk/blog/2011/12/06/5-stages-of-workplace -learning-revisited.

Deterding, S. (2013). "Cultivating Ludus: The Rhetorics of Gamification." Presented at Gamification 2013, University of Waterloo, Stratford, Ontario, Canada, October 4, www.slideshare.net/dings.

Dirksen, J. (2012). *Design for How People Learn*. Berkeley, CA: New Riders.

Duarte, N. (2008). *slide:ology: The Art and Science of Creating Great Presentations*. Sebastopol, CA: O'Reilly Media.

Garner, R., M.G. Gillingham, and C.S. White. (1989). "Effects of 'Seductive Details' on Macroprocessing and Microprocessing in Adults and Children." *Cognition and Instruction* 6:41-57.

Gartner. (2013). "Gartner's 2013 Hype Cycle for Emerging Technologies Maps Out Evolving Relationship Between Humans and Machines." Press release, August 19, Stamford, CT.

Hart, J. (2013). "Learning in the Workplace Survey." *Learning in the Social Workplace* (blog), Centre for Learning and Performance Technologies, April 22, www.c4lpt.co.uk/blog/2013/04/22/company-training-of-little-value.

Heath, C., and D. Heath. (2008). *Made to Stick: Why Some Ideas Survive and Others Die*. New York: Random House.

Jarche, H. (2012). "Work Is Learning and Learning Is Work." *Life in Perpetual Beta* (blog), June 17, www.jarche.com/2012/06/work-is-learning-and-learning-is-the-work.

Kapp, K.M. (2007). *Gadgets, Games, and Gizmos for Learning*. San Francisco: Pfeiffer.

Keller, J.M. (2006). "What Is Motivational Design?" ARCSMODEL.COM, June, www.arcsmodel.com/#!motivational-design/c2275.

Kineo. "Learning Models: Useful Blueprints for eLearning Designers." www.kineo.com/m/0/elearning-design-v2.pdf.

Kineo. (2013). "Avoiding the Trap of Clicky-Clicky Bling-Bling." www.kineo.com/m/0/clicky-click-hr.pdf.

Kohn, A. (2013). "Brain and Memory: Seven Tips That Improve E-Learning." Presented at ASTD 2013 Tech Knowledge, San Jose, CA, January 29.

Kuhlmann, T. (2009). "Should You Add Background Audio to Your E-Learning Courses?" *The Rapid E-Learning Blog*, December 1, www.articulate.com/rapid-elearning/should-you-add-background-audio-to-your-e-learning-courses.

Learning Theories Knowledgebase. (2009). "ARCS Model of Motivational Design (Keller)." www.learning-theories.com/kellers-arcs-model-of-motivational -design.html.

Medina, J. (2008). *Brain Rules: 12 Principles for Surviving and Thriving at Work, Home, and School*. Seattle, WA: Pear Press.

Merrill, M.D. (2009). "First Principles of Instruction." In I*nstructional Design Theories and Models: Building a Common Knowledge Base*, vol. 3, edited by C.M. Reigeluth and A. Carr (New York: Routledge Publishers), http://mdavidmerrill .com/Papers/FirstPrinciplesReigeluthCarr.pdf.

Merrill, M.D., L. Drake, M.J. Lacy, J. Pratt, and ID2 Research Group. (1996). "Reclaiming Instructional Design." *Educational Technology* 36(5): 5-7, http:// mdavidmerrill.com/Papers/Reclaiming.PDF.

Moore, C. (2010). "The Big Mistake in Elearning." *Cathy Moore: Let's Save the World From Boring Training!* (blog), May 10, http://blog.cathy-moore.com.

Moore, C. (2007). "Turn Objectives into Motivators," *Cathy Moore: Let's Save the World From Boring Training!* (blog), December 19, http://blog.cathy-moore .com/2007/12/makeover-turn-objectives-into-motivators/.

Quinn, C. (2006). "Making it Matter to the Learner: e-Motional e-Learning." *Learning Solutions Magazine*, April 3, www.learningsolutionsmag.com /articles/228/making-it-matter-to-the-learner-e-motional-e-learning.

Quinn, C. (2013). "Yes, You Do Have to Change." *Learnlets* (blog), March 18, http:// blog.learnlets.com/?p=3232.

Thalheimer, W. (2010). "How Much Do People Forget?" Work-Learning Research, http://willthalheimer.typepad.com/files/how-much-do-people -forget-v12-14-2010.pdf.

Thalheimer, W. (2006). "New Taxonomy for Learning Objectives," *Will at Work Learning* (blog), June 1, www.willatworklearning.com/2006/06/new_taxonomy _fo.html.

Thalheimer, W. (2004). "Bells, Whistles, Neon, and Purple Prose: When Interesting Words, Sounds, and Visuals Hurt Learning and Performance—A Review of the Seductive-Augmentation Research." Work-Learning Research, www.oktopusz .hu/domain9/files/modules/module15/28283C732CAE682.pdf.

Tracey, R. (2010). "Taxonomy of Learning Theories." *E-Learning Provocateur* (blog), January 12, http://ryan2point0.wordpress.com/2010/01/12/taxonomy -of-learning-theories.

Tugend, A. (2012). "Praise Is Fleeting, but Brickbats We Recall." *New York Times*, March 23, www.nytimes.com/2012/03/24/your-money/why-people-remember -negative-events-more-than-positive-ones.html.

Wagner, E. (2011). "Essay: In Search of the Secret Handshakes of ID." *Journal of Applied Instructional Design* 1(1): 33-37, www.jaidpub.org/wp-content /uploads/2011/03/EssayWagnerApr2011.pdf.

Ward, M. (2010). "What Is Design?" *Echo Enduring Blog*, May 25, http://blog .echoenduring.com/2010/05/25/what-is-design.

Weinschenk, S. (2011). *100 Things Every Designer Needs to Know about People.* Berkeley, CA: New Riders.

About the Author

 Cammy Bean has been collaborating with organizations to design online learning programs since 1996. She is the VP of learning design for Kineo, a global provider of technology-based learning solutions. An acclaimed public speaker, Cammy gets fired up about instructional design, avoiding the trap of clicky-clicky bling-bling, and ways to use technology to create real behavior change. She writes the blog, *Learning Visions* (www.cammybean .kineo.com), and can be found on Twitter @cammybean.

About the Author

Index